Coping with Age-related Memory Loss

Dr Tom Smith has been writing full time since 1977, after spending six years in general practice and seven years in medical research. He writes regularly for medical journals and magazines and has often featured on BBC Radio Scotland.

Since September 2006 he has written the 'Doctor, Doctor' column in the *Guardian* Saturday magazine. He also has columns in the *Bradford Telegraph and Argus*, the *Lancashire Telegraph* and the *Galloway* and *Carrick Gazettes*. His other books for Sheldon Press include *Heart Attacks: Prevent and Survive*, *Living with Alzheimer's Disease*, *Coping Successfully with Prostate Cancer*, *Overcoming Back Pain*, *Coping with Bowel Cancer* and *Coping with Heartburn and Reflux*. He has recently broken into medical humour with *Doctor, Have You Got a Minute?*, and his stories of his early years in practice were published in April 2007 under the title *Doctor by the Shore* (Short Books).

He still practises as a locum for his friends in general practice in south-west Scotland.

D1350690

Overcoming Common Problems Series

Selected titles

A full list of titles is available from Sheldon Press,
36 Causton Street, London SW1P 4ST and on our website at
www.sheldonpress.co.uk

Living with Loss and Grief
Julia Tugendhat

Living with Lupus
Philippa Pigache

Living with Nut Allergies
Karen Evennett

Living with Osteoarthritis
Dr Patricia Gilbert

Living with Osteoporosis
Dr Joan Gomez

Living with Rheumatoid Arthritis
Philippa Pigache

Living with a Seriously Ill Child
Dr Jan Aldridge

Living with Sjögren's Syndrome
Sue Dyson

Losing a Baby
Sarah Ewing

Losing a Child
Linda Hurcombe

Making Friends with Your Stepchildren
Rosemary Wells

Making Relationships Work
Alison Waines

Overcoming Anger
Dr Windy Dryden

Overcoming Anxiety
Dr Windy Dryden

Overcoming Back Pain
Dr Tom Smith

Overcoming Depression
Dr Windy Dryden and Sarah Opie

Overcoming Hurt
Dr Windy Dryden

Overcoming Jealousy
Dr Windy Dryden

Overcoming Loneliness and Making Friends
Márianna Csóti

Overcoming Procrastination
Dr Windy Dryden

Overcoming Shame
Dr Windy Dryden

Rheumatoid Arthritis
Mary-Claire Mason and Dr Elaine Smith

Simplify Your Life
Naomi Saunders

Ten Steps to Positive Living
Dr Windy Dryden

The Assertiveness Handbook
Mary Hartley

The Candida Diet Book
Karen Brody

The Chronic Fatigue Healing Diet
Christine Craggs-Hinton

The Depression Diet Book
Theresa Cheung

The Fibromyalgia Healing Diet
Christine Craggs-Hinton

The Irritable Bowel Diet Book
Rosemary Nicol

The Multiple Sclerosis Diet Book
Tessa Buckley

The PMS Diet Book
Karen Evennett

The PMS Handbook
Theresa Cheung

The Self-Esteem Journal
Alison Waines

The Thinking Person's Guide to Happiness
Ruth Searle

The Traveller's Good Health Guide
Dr Ted Lankester

Think Your Way to Happiness
Dr Windy Dryden and Jack Gordon

Treat Your Own Knees
Jim Johnson

Treating Arthritis Diet Book
Margaret Hills

Treating Arthritis Exercise Book
Margaret Hills and Janet Horwood

Treating Arthritis – The Drug-Free Way
Margaret Hills

Understanding Obsessions and Compulsions
Dr Frank Tallis

When Someone You Love Has Depression
Barbara Baker

Your Man's Health
Fiona Marshall

Overcoming Common Problems

Coping with Age-related Memory Loss

TOM SMITH

First published in Great Britain in 2007

Sheldon Press
36 Causton Street
London SW1P 4ST

British Library Cataloguing-in-Publication Data
A catalogue record for this book is available from the British Library

ISBN 978-0-85969-994-5

1 3 5 7 9 10 8 6 4 2

Typeset by Fakenham Photosetting Ltd
Printed in Great Britain by Ashford Colour Press

Contents

Introduction

We all experience instances of memory loss. It's not long, in any conversation between normal adults, before one of them admits to an inability to recall a simple name. It's popularly called a 'senior moment' or a 'CRAFT' (Can't Remember A Flaming Thing) episode. Yet, after a few minutes, when we have moved on to another subject and are not thinking about it, the forgotten word pops up into our consciousness.

We all do it, no matter how well we have been educated and how much we try to 'train' ourselves to keep our memory alive and flourishing. We don't have to be old for it to happen to us: I have had a 'forgettory' rather than a memory since I was a student. I'm fine with medical names and facts, but outside my job? When mixing socially, I can't put a name to a face. I have always mixed them up, to the regular embarrassment of my long-suffering wife. Why does this happen? It's only recently that we have begun to understand our brains and how they form, retain and use our memory banks – and how we might lose them.

That's what this book is about. It's not about dementia, yet every time we go through a phase of poor memory we naturally think that this is what is facing us. Dementia is a combination of forgetting and loss of intellect: it's a one-way street, with no recovery. Temporary memory loss is a natural process that we can deal with and, to some extent, reverse.

How we can best keep our memory sharp has been the subject of hundreds of books, usually written by people who have made a living from prodigious feats of memory on the stage or in the media, or by those wishing to hone their readers' business skills. If you are old enough to remember Leslie Welsh, Britain's first radio 'Memory Man', you will know what I mean. He would reel off the names of every player in every English Cup Final for the previous century, and was never caught out by the trickiest of questions sent in by listeners.

Today's 'memory men' (almost all male) can remember the sequence of cards in a stack of several shuffled packs, after glancing through them just once. Yet the rest of us can hardly remember a phone number. What have they got that we haven't – and can we learn to do it? If we can, does it really improve our memories for everyday things? Will it stop us having senior moments or CRAFT?

More important still, will it prevent us from developing dementia, such as Alzheimer's disease? I suspect that most people who buy this book have a fear in the back of their minds of developing this condition. So, we will dispose of this fear immediately: memory loss on its own is not dementia; it's a normal feature of life as we pack more information into our brains. The longer we live, the more difficult it is to retain and bring back to our consciousness our memories. That's partly because we are constantly filling our brain's reserves with new memories, or new data, and that inevitably means that some of the older or less used memories are more difficult to bring up into our consciousness. They are still there, but access to them takes a little longer. We are not really suffering serious memory loss, but experiencing a 'data jam'. At 60 we have vastly more memories than we had at 30, so it's unavoidable that we 'lose' a few on the way.

The book starts with two case histories: you will probably recognize yourself in the first. If you identify with the second, you need to take your memory loss more seriously, and see your doctor about it. They are chosen as examples of different types of memory loss, with perhaps different causes, to illustrate the way the brain works. It gives examples of when memory loss is normal, and when we should suspect that it might be becoming abnormal. It then explains what we know so far about the physical side of memory loss – how the brain collects, stores and brings back to mind our memories – and continues with how research today is finding out much more about it.

That leads to the ways doctors may investigate loss of memory if they think there is something wrong. Of course, for some people memory loss may be the start of more serious mental illness, and how we identify these people takes up a whole chapter. There are standard memory tests, examples of which are given, that help us to do so.

Most of the book is then devoted to improving our memories. Like taking on a course of physical exercise for the first time, improving your memory is difficult to begin with. Happily, it gets easier as you continue with it, and as you can practise it every day, just sitting in your favourite chair, it doesn't take so much physical effort. Mental effort, however, is a *must*. If you don't use your brain, you stand a much higher chance of losing it. It's no coincidence that the more educated you are, the more likely you are to fend off memory loss and dementia, and the longer you will live. So keeping your brain active is the number one priority. How to do this is explained in the book.

1

Two case histories

James is 67 and has been a family doctor all his adult life. Over the years he has come to be known throughout his community, and he knows most of the people in the small town in which he practised. While he was working, he could name every one of them, and could probably list their family tree too. He has been retired for two years, and gradually things have changed.

Now, once in a while, when people greet him in the street, he can't remember their names. They all know exactly who he is, of course, but he can't bring their names quickly to mind. Which is embarrassing, because if he is walking along, say, with his wife, he can't introduce them to her. Naturally, he is concerned about this. Could he be 'losing it'?

Once he does recall their names, usually a few minutes after they have gone on their respective ways, he remembers everything about them. Their medical histories come flooding back, along with the details of their families and their troubles. But by then it's too late: they are by now a hundred yards away, and it wouldn't be seemly to chase after them.

James also has difficulties with remembering other names – such as those of celebrities in the media, musicians, or politicians who made the headlines a few years before, but have since faded from the limelight. He is still 'on the ball' when it comes to naming people who are currently in the spotlight, and he remembers those who were vitally important to him when he was much younger, such as his medical school professors or classmates. He has no difficulties with people he sees every day, or even distant relatives he hasn't seen for years, but he has trouble remembering the names and faces of people to whom he has recently been introduced.

His worry is that he might be starting to deteriorate mentally, yet he still does 'brain' puzzles every day (he loves cryptic crosswords and the difficult Sudoku in his daily paper). And he still reads his medical journals every week with interest and understanding, although he tends to concentrate on medical news rather than medical politics. He can remember all his medical facts, old and new, with the sharpness he had as a student.

James was so worried about his memory loss that he asked me, as a colleague, to test him for impending dementia. James and I, and our wives, have known each other for many years, so I thought it sensible to ask James's wife to come along too. After all, if he was beginning to 'lose it', as he put it, his wife would need to be prepared for the future.

I needn't have worried. He was certainly his old bright, intelligent and humorous self, and showed no signs of dementia. When I brought him back from the office into our lounge, and the four of us talked over his case, his wife began to laugh. He had kept her in the dark about why he wanted to see me, and this was the first time she had heard of his concerns.

She told us that this wasn't new. When they had married 40 years before, she soon found out that he had difficulty on social occasions. He would mix up faces and names, and she had long ago decided that the best approach to this was to tolerate it, and for her to be the 'social memory' for them both. She didn't think that he had actually got much worse than he had been so many years before. He, on the other hand, because he was no longer seeing his patients on a regular basis, had for the first time become truly aware of how bad his 'social memory' was. After two years away from the medical scene, the names that were so familiar to him on a daily basis were slipping from his immediate memory. He hadn't been used to this when working, but his wife hadn't been surprised by it.

Neither was my wife. She told them both about my 'forget-tory' – a name she has had for many years for my poor memory. I explained that I was in absolutely the same boat as James, and had to work very hard to recall the names of people I had treated in previous years.

In fact, it's worse for me, because I do regular 'locum' days in different practices in my region of Scotland. This means that I see people only for ten-minute appointments, and often never again. If I meet them in the street or socially afterwards, I hardly ever remember them. Sometimes, even when they have come back for a repeat appointment, I need to look at their notes beforehand to recall who they are. Often it's their medical condition and what I have written down on the previous occasion, and not their appearance, which reminds me that I've met them before. It can make for an awkward first few minutes in the surgery before I have brought my memories of that previous consultation into full focus and am fully comfortable with the patient and his or her problem.

James was mightily relieved, and we began to discuss memory problems and what we might do about it. In fact, the idea for this book arose out of that evening's conversation.

Arthur's case was more disturbing. I've known him for over thirty years. He lives in the next village to ours, and retired three years ago from his lifelong job as head gardener to a big estate. For many years he was in huge demand as a speaker at local garden club meetings. His knowledge of horticulture was encyclopaedic: he knew every Latin name and could talk about any plant that could be grown outside, inside and in greenhouses in our area. He would advise us on what might be suitable for our coastal, river valley and mountain gardens (we have them all in our part of western Scotland), and was never at a loss.

I hadn't seen Arthur for a year when I met him in our local village shop. He was carrying a shopping list, and he handed it over the counter to the assistant, who then went around the shelves to fill his basket. We said hello, and he smiled at me warmly.

'How did your wife get on with that tree?' he asked. 'You know, the one that forms a canopy and has long pod fruits? I never thought it would grow here.'

He was talking of an Indian bean tree, or catalpa, that we had planted in our garden four years before. It soon became obvious that he had forgotten its names – not just the Latin name, but the English one, too. That worried me, because the Arthur I had known just one year before would never have done this.

'It's doing well,' I replied. 'You should come over to see it.'

'Oh, I'm not out and about as I used to be,' he said. 'It might be a bit difficult.'

At that point his basket was brought to him. The assistant wrote the bill total into a book that she had taken from under the counter and he walked out. I watched him go the fifty yards or so to his home, and felt desperately sorry for him. Our house was well known to him, and he and his wife had to pass our front door on many days in a normal week, so dropping in on us would not have been a problem. That book under the counter, too, suggested that he might not be trusted with money. There had to be something wrong.

I phoned Elizabeth, his wife, that evening, and was sad to hear that his memory had drastically deteriorated over the previous few weeks: she told me that his doctor was investigating him for early dementia, and she was very distressed about him.

What was the essential difference between James and Arthur? For James, the social memories were not particularly important, so that he had no real drive to remember them. However, ask him about the essentials in his life, and he would say that his knowledge of medicine took priority. He took the trouble every day to refresh his store of knowledge by reading his journals and regularly attended clinical meetings with other doctors. If there was something he wanted to know, he would look it up on the internet. There are special sites for doctors, and James regularly looked at them, often testing himself for fun in the various quizzes set to keep younger doctors up to date. Though he was no longer young in years, he was still young at heart where medicine was concerned.

James had not forgotten the basics of his profession: Arthur had. For Arthur to have forgotten the name of a tree would have been as bad as James forgetting the name of the tonsils or appendix. Arthur's loss was serious, as it indicated other problems in the brain – and Elizabeth confirmed them.

Thankfully, there's a happy postscript to this story. Two months after that meeting in the shop I met Arthur again. It was the day of the village church fair, and he was going great guns advising people on their plant problems. I was astonished at the change in him. He was bright and cheerful, and I listened as he explained the details of some obscure disease of pear trees to a local gardener. The names and their relevance were all there, as if he had never lost them.

I caught up with him at the end of the afternoon, and he explained what had happened. When I had met him before, he was in the throes of a severe chest infection. He had been coughing and breathless for about a month, and had felt generally unwell, physically weak and mentally listless. He 'couldn't be bothered' with things, and he admitted that he had been 'down' mentally.

Shortly after our first meeting, Arthur's doctor had started him on a high dose of antibiotics for his chest infection. The change had been dramatic. His chest cleared up within four days, and he felt much better. His joy in life returned, and his memory and interests flooded back. He was soon in demand again, and Elizabeth had her old Arthur back. It turned out that my assumption about his money problems had been wrong, too. Arthur and Elizabeth had had an arrangement with the shopkeeper for many years about paying for the groceries monthly. I reflected on how wrong speculations could be, and was happy for them both that there was no underlying sinister reason for him not handling money.

Arthur was not dementing: his physical illness – the chest infection – not only made him feel physically low, but had made him severely depressed mentally as well. Once the offending germ had been dealt with, his mental state improved just as much as his physical one. He began to make the effort to recall things, and they came to the surface again. He hadn't forgotten anything – the difference was that, with his depression lifted, he was able to use his memory-recall system again. It isn't always essential to be physically or mentally fit to retain a good memory, but Arthur's case certainly suggests that they are both a big help.

2

How the brain remembers

How is it that we remember things? Where are our memories, and how do we go about storing them and recalling them? How do we know if they are true, or mixed up with what we have been told later about something? Do we remember things best as children, or as young adults? Do we stop remembering new things, or discard some memories, as we get older? Are there particular memories that we treat differently from others? Do we continue to recall memories accurately as the years pass? Is a poor memory related to the loss of actual memories, or do our memories remain stored in the brain, but are sometimes impossible to bring back into our consciousness? In other words, is this book really about loss of memory, or is it about a difficulty in bringing back into our consciousness memories that are still lodged in our brains, and not forgotten? Is all we need a quiet moment, and perhaps a different way of approaching how we recall our memories, to bring them to light?

How the brain organizes our experiences

To try to answer these various questions we need to know a bit about how the brain works. First of all we need an intact brain that can organize all our experiences – what we see, hear, feel and taste – into areas from which we can recall them at will. It uses a network of nerve cells intercommunicating with electrical impulses and chemical 'transmitters' all over the surface of the brain – the 'cortex'. It also needs a central 'control room' deep in the middle of the brain, called the hippocampus (so called because the early anatomists thought it looked like a sea-horse).

For many years the accepted wisdom about memory storage was that the nerve impulses that arrive in the brain from our eyes, ears, nose, tongue, skin, joints, muscles and gut are collected in the hippocampus as a sort of 'hard disk'. The hippocampus was then thought to send these impulses to be stored in the cortex as the equivalent of data on 'floppy disks' or DVDs, that we can, at some time in the future, dredge up at will.

We no longer think that this is what happens. Each memory is thought to be the result of a pattern of electrical impulses and chemical changes over the whole surface of the brain that is 'tapped into' and 're-run' when we remember things. Essentially, we re-run exactly the same pattern that was laid down in the brain when we first experienced the circumstances that we are remembering. It's thought that dreams are a random flickering of electrical circuits and chemical transmitters through the 'memory' cortex. They are bizarre because they wander 'off piste', so to speak, giving us memories of experiences that we have never had. It may be that the hallucinations of schizophrenia have a similar origin.

We still accept, however, that the hippocampus is vital to retaining a good memory. Several examples spring to mind.

The big hippocampus ...

The first is evidence from London taxi drivers. London's streets are named and laid out at random. Unlike, for example, New York, they are not numbered, and the names are not allocated (as are the Big Apple's avenues and streets) according to the direction in which they run. Therefore learning the street map of London is a prodigious feat of memory. It's called (as everyone in Britain surely knows) 'The Knowledge'. London cabbies have to study The Knowledge for three or four years before they can take the test that allows them a licence to carry passengers. The test is amazingly rigorous, with many questions about routes from one part of the city to another. Failing is not an option for them – if they don't have The Knowledge, they can't be a cabbie.

The fascinating thing about learning The Knowledge is that it develops the hippocampus. London cabbies are a breed apart and they are great people to chat to. Their memories are not just developed to take in the street map of London – they seem to have a pretty good handle on many other subjects, too. Their knowledge of the details of current affairs, such as politics, the media, football and sports in general, is wide and accurate – though their opinions on them vary as much as any other group's.

Cabbies are also willing to put themselves at the disposal of medical researchers, which is why doctors were fascinated, in 2005, to read of scans of cabbies' brains. Their hippocampuses (or hippocampi – language experts can argue for hours on the correct plural!) are much larger and more active than other people's. Not only that, the study showed that their hippocampuses almost certainly started off just like everyone else's, but grew and became more efficient as they learned The Knowledge. The more experienced the cabbie, the more effectively their brains could organize their memories, and the more streets, roads and avenues they could recall. That is fair enough, you might think. The more we read maps, the better we should be able to orientate ourselves in a city like London. And why shouldn't the area of brain involved develop accordingly? What was *not* expected was that it isn't just the map-reading skills that improved in the cabbies. There was good evidence that their general intelligence improved too.

One part of that evidence comes from the success of a London cabbie a few years ago in winning the final of Britain's television programme called *Mastermind*. It may have surprised the viewing public, but it didn't surprise the memory experts. *Mastermind* is well known in Britain as the quiz show that really sorts out the clever from the rest. Contestants have to pass through several rounds of searching questions on particular subjects and on general knowledge before reaching the final. In each round they have to choose a different specialist subject: that's half the programme. In the second half, they have to demonstrate their general knowledge. As the programme progresses towards the final rounds, the questions become ever more difficult to answer, so that the final four contestants have proved themselves extremely well versed in several specialist subjects and to have an encyclopaedic knowledge of everything else. It is without doubt the hardest quiz show on television.

One would expect 'Masterminds', therefore, to have a good formal education at least to university level. On the contrary, many successful *Mastermind* contestants are self-taught. Regardless of whether they left school at 16 or, conversely, took a postgraduate degree, what they really have in common is an insatiable curiosity and desire to amass facts. But even these qualities aren't enough. They also need a system by which they can organize their data into 'packages' so that they can easily bring them back to mind. Each contestant has a different way of doing this, but they all have one. Without it, they wouldn't get past the initial interview stage for the programme. Learning The Knowledge forces cabbies to organize their brainpower so that they can memorize to perfection thousands of seemingly disconnected names and landmarks. In doing that, they are honing all aspects of memory, and arguably their intellect too. It's the perfect background for winning *Mastermind*.

If there is one thing that the cabbies can tell us, it's that memory isn't what we *have*, but what we *do*. They have had to work hard to develop their memories, and work equally hard to maintain them. They see memory as something they work on, not on something that is innate within them. It's a good start for anyone trying to improve his or her memory. Most of us don't need to keep the cabbie's stack of facts in our memories, but even for everyday living, we need a lot more than we might think. Later on in the book, in the section on prospective memory, I'll come back to that.

.. and the small hippocampus

A well-developed hippocampus is a great advantage for a good memory, and the converse, a damaged hippocampus, has a striking effect on it.

Harry

Born prematurely in a small village many miles from his regional hospital, it was more than a day before Harry could be placed in an incubator and given the expert attention he needed to help him breathe properly. He survived and grew into a happy, apparently normal boy. Yet at school his teachers found that he was having difficulty in learning tasks that other children took in their stride. He seemed to be bright enough, with good skills in numbers and in language: his grammar and spelling abilities were good for his age. His knowledge of the world around him was excellent, and he was just as interested as the rest of his schoolmates in the things that children like to do.

He had no difficulty in completing memory tests (see the digit span test below) provided he was asked to do so immediately. But ask him half an hour later to repeat the result, and he would fail completely. His parents had started to worry about him when they realized that he could not remember, even for a few minutes, things that were essential to the normal running of his life. On a visit with them to a friend's house, when his mother took him to the toilet, he could not find his way back to the lounge where his parents were. This rang alarm bells, and it was only when he was taken to see a professor of paediatric neurology that the full extent of what he had lost became apparent.

Harry's memory was much worse than his parents had thought. He was unable to recall most of his past: for example, he could not remember holidays, where he had been, when and with whom. Especially distressing to his parents, he had also lost memories of his emotions – sadness, joy, anger or other feelings – that we all feel are strongly involved in our memories. Harry's memories, such as they were,

were related only to facts: he could not recall or re-live the emotions he felt when he acquired them. His parents took to carrying their camera everywhere they went, and showed him afterwards, repeatedly, where they had been, and talked to him about how the family, and he in particular, felt at the time.

The professor's investigations pinpointed the trouble, in that brain scans showed that Harry had a severely underdeveloped hippocampus. It had been the part of his brain most affected by the lack of oxygen. From then on, Harry and his parents were on a steep learning curve, to try to improve his memory so that he could live as normal a life as an adult as possible. His ordinary intelligence has helped him a lot – he is living proof that intelligence and memory are not one and the same – in that he has insight into his problems.

He understands what he has lost, and is always trying to 'get round' his difficulties. Visit his house, or his workplace (he is a greenkeeper at a golf course), and you will see lots of stickers hung around the walls telling him his order of tasks for the day. He is a wizard at computer games, but he has to re-learn the rules of each game over and over again, as he forgets them too easily. If he wants to watch a programme on television, he still has to ask his family to remind him that it's on, and even what it's about, or otherwise he will forget about it. Yet he is not downhearted. Now that he knows he has a gap in his memory mechanisms, he is doing all he can to fill it with practical mechanisms to get round it.

Then there's the cortex …

So the hippocampus – the cabbie's forte and Harry's loss – is the basis for receiving new memories, but it's only the beginning of the story. What other parts of the brain do we need to keep a good memory? My next example, Jane's case, helps to provide the answer.

Jane

A brilliant medical student, Jane passed all her exams easily. She had what she now describes as a 'photographic memory'. She says that when she was studying, all she needed to do to remember what she was reading was to take a mental 'snapshot' of the page. She would then be able to recall that page for her exam, and pick out the relevant paragraphs in writing her answers.

I remember my own student days of trying to read textbooks. At my very best I could only read around ten pages an hour, and even then I would have to go over them twice or three times to try to drill the facts into my head. My own memory was far from photographic. Faced with an examination question, it would have been hopeless for me to try to bring in front of my mental eyes the pages I had read. For me, the best way was to remember the logic of what I had read, and to try to reproduce that in my own words. Obviously Jane and I had very different systems of recall.

Looking back over the lives of the two of us, I was definitely the lucky one. I've been fortunate with my health, and still use my memory systems in the same way as when I was a student. Jane's life has been very different.

Two years after she graduated as a doctor, with a brilliant career before her, she suffered her first stroke. Unknown to her, she had been born with an abnormal blood vessel in the left half of her brain. She was 25 years old when it 'leaked' blood into the tissues around it, causing her to lose consciousness. When she came round, she couldn't speak, had no idea where her right arm and leg were, and could not recognize the faces of her friends and family.

She still retained her intellect, and she used that, along with huge determination, over the next two years, to learn to speak again. She has never regained the sensation in her right leg and arm, but has trained herself to cope with the loss. She has done this so well that no one meeting her today, nearly thirty years later, would suspect that anything was wrong. She can walk her dogs and drive her car, and a casual observer would think that she had no problems at all.

Jane was doubly unfortunate. The initial stroke had already damaged her brain, but the abnormal blood vessel was still a threat. If it bled again, the next stroke would probably have been fatal. So the surgeons had to remove what they could of the critical blood vessel. That meant extensive brain surgery, removing not just the abnormal area, but some of the surrounding brain, too. She was then protected against any more strokes, but in the process lost what she had treasured the most – her photographic memory.

Now Jane has to use all sorts of memory 'tricks' to remember facts, faces and names, and she still finds it frustrating, nearly thirty years on. She struggles at times to remember everyday words, although she is acutely aware that they are there, somewhere in her brain. She explains that she knows that the memories are still in her brain, but that she no longer has access to them. During the operation, the surgeons found that the abnormal vessel extended into her cortex, and they had to remove some of it to ensure her safety. That, it appears, was the crucial step to her loss of memory.

Over the years, Jane has done for her memory what she did initially for her loss of body image and speech. She has built up her memory banks again, presumably using different areas of cortex than those she used before her operation. She still stumbles over familiar words, but she has become much better at 'finding' them over the years. Only her closest friends know how much she has lost, and how much effort she puts into using speech to communicate with others. It's easier for her to write because the part of the brain she has always used for the written word has not been affected by her stroke or surgery.

Obviously, Jane couldn't continue with her career as a full-time family doctor. She has, however, become a renowned medical hypnotherapist, working with hospital colleagues to treat people with pain and to help with anaesthesia. She uses her skills in a unique way to help herself, in a form of self-hypnosis, and I am sure that this determination has helped her to use parts of her brain as substitute centres of memory for those that she lost. I have huge admiration for her, and I use her case to show that even with devastating brain damage, some of a person's memory loss can be retrieved. To do it successfully, however, requires a lot of effort and steely determination and persistence.

... and loss of the language centre

Morag

A third example is Morag. Her case is another example of how a brain injury can lead to loss of memory that somehow can be 'got round' with time. She was born on the Isle of Mull, off the west coast of Scotland, and for the first five years of her life she spoke the first language of her parents and older sisters – Gaelic. Scots Gaelic, like Irish, is a language quite unlike English in its construction and its consonants and vowel sounds. It's only spoken today by some 100,000 people, so although it's a beautiful language, especially for music and poetry, it isn't practical as an everyday language when you grow up. So every Gaelic-speaker learns English, too.

Morag's first brush with the English language came when she started school. She learned it as a second language, much as Dutch school-children learn English (do you know any Dutch people who can't speak English fluently?), and soon became expert in it. She was so expert, in fact, that she eventually became an English teacher and author, writing short stories and articles in the educational press. Eventually she retired, and enjoyed a few years in her house and garden near the city in which she had taught. Although she visited the islands of her childhood regularly, she decided not to go back there to live, and she rarely used her Gaelic.

In her late seventies, Morag started to have small strokes, and bit by bit her memory deteriorated, so that by her mid-eighties she was hardly speaking to her friends and neighbours. Eventually she had to enter a nursing home, where she was thought to be rapidly dementing, forgetting her past as a teacher and saying little to her nurses and carers.

One day a new nurse joined the staff. She hailed from the Isle of Lewis, and she too had learned Gaelic as a child. Reading Morag's notes, she tried her Gaelic on her. To her amazement, Morag became animated and excited for the first time in two years. She was able to converse easily in Gaelic, and obviously could think, reason and remember her life with considerable accuracy. She would even correct her nurse's 'Lewis Gaelic'. Morag had retained her teacher's penchant for correction of grammar – and, in her view, Lewis Gaelic was not as correct or 'pure' as the Mull form of the language. Morag had lost her English – but not her first language.

Today she still speaks in Gaelic to the staff, and is being encouraged to re-learn her English all over again. It's difficult for her, because her small strokes appear to have taken away much of the area of brain needed to learn a second language. But her first language is still there – proof, if we need it, that the area of the brain we use as babies to learn to speak our native tongue is separate from the one we use at school to learn a new one.

When your memories are false

Losing your memory after a brain injury is bad enough, but it's much worse if, when you recover, you have a whole lot of new memories that are false – you are certain that you remember, in detail, occasions and circumstances that never happened.

Throughout August 2006, BBC Radio 4 broadcast a series of programmes on memory. Its presenter, Mariella Frostrup, claimed to have a poor memory herself, although I'm sure she was being modest. She seemed to me to be very much 'on the ball'. It was an excellent series, and it's now on the BBC website at <BBC.co.uk/memory>. Most of the programmes concentrated on normal memory in people with no health problems, to show how we use it in normal life. The website is a comprehensive review of the programme and its background material, and I wholeheartedly recommend it as a great help to people wanting to know more about their memory and how they might improve it.

Charles

One of the programmes, broadcast on Radio 4 on 16 August 2006, highlighted the case of Charles, a 46-year-old mining engineer, who some years before had been badly injured. Asked about the experience, he remembered that he had read in a trade magazine an article written by a man who was selling, cut-price, illicit raw diamonds to jewellers. There was even a photograph of the man in the journal to accompany the article. Seeing this man by chance in a shop, Charles had challenged him, then followed him out of the shop door. On the pavement he had been run down by a getaway car, and his head had smashed against the kerb, severely injuring his brain.

The story sounded feasible enough until his wife Cathy told her version of it. Far from being an international criminal, the man had been a drug-fuelled smash-and-grab petty thief, and when Charles had run out into the street to confront him, he had been knocked down.

So how could Charles have got the story so wrong? In the 2006 interview, several years after the event, he still insisted on the radio that he had indeed read the article and confronted the man because he had recognized his face. He said on air that one day he would find the article to prove he was correct.

Charles had another false memory. He was convinced that he had had lunch with his grandfather only the previous year – yet he had died more than twenty years before. The memory of the lunch had persisted, but had been misplaced in the wrong time.

Dr Gail Robinson, a specialist neurosurgeon, explained what had happened. She said that Charles had suffered damage to the frontal (above and behind the eyes) and temporal (next to the temples and ears) areas of cerebral cortex – the frontal and temporal 'lobes'. She explained that memories are first collected by the temporal lobes, and when they need to be retrieved into our consciousness the frontal lobes do the job. With damage to both regions, Charles's memory of events is distorted. He may have read a piece in a journal about a fraudster, but his brain had mixed it up with the robbery, and this has been fixed as a permanent memory in his brain. The article may not have existed at all: the false memory may be similar to a dream, in which random electrical impulses produced this false experience.

The problem in Charles's case is the frontal lobe damage. The frontal lobes monitor how real memories are, and when they are uninjured and working normally, they can reject false memories. This isn't the case for Charles. When he first recovered consciousness, weeks after his injury, he had lost his memories of his childhood and did not recognize his wife and children. Gradually, most of his memory has returned, showing that the brain has great powers of recovery, but it's not complete. His persistent belief that his grandfather was still alive and that he had recently had lunch with him still worries him. Rationalizing, Charles accepts that he would now be over a hundred years old, but he still finds it difficult to come to terms with what is a real memory for him.

Psychiatrists and neurologists call this feeling, that a false memory is true, 'confabulation'. In the programme, Charles made it clear that he didn't like the word, feeling that it suggested he was 'making up' his memories, and that this was akin to lying. Dr Robinson stressed that this was not the case. She said that 'confabulation is convincing, clear, logical and rational' and that it could be presented as fact extraordinarily well. Because patients really believe it, it is not dishonesty.

How will Charles manage to come to terms with these false memories? One way is to discuss them with someone who was present at the time of the supposed memory, so as to reinforce the correction. He has worked hard with a rehabilitation unit and with his wife, Cathy, who provides him with the correct information about any memories that they have shared. It's hard for them both. She has to keep correcting him, and he finds it very difficult to ditch a memory that he knows is true 'because I have seen this with my own eyes'. Every time he discusses a specific memory – such as the incident of the injury or the meal with his grandfather – the wrong memory is further embedded in his brain, and it's more difficult for him to reject it, and believe the true version.

'Is my memory what other people are telling me what my memory should be?' he still asks. 'Can't other people's memories be jumbled up?' He makes a good point.

I include these case histories as an encouragement to people who think that they are 'losing it' to accept that all isn't lost. This is true even for Charles, with his extensive brain damage. Many people, if they make the effort, can recover much of the memory that they used to have, if they can find the key to unlocking it.

Even if you don't think your memory is too bad, and you have no health problems, with no brain damage, there are still ways to improve it.

3

Normal memory – how it works

Let's assume you have a normal brain, with all the areas of it that are concerned with memory being healthy and working as they should. Think of it as two large spheres, the 'cerebral hemispheres' connected in the centre by a 'bridge' of communicating fibres. Deep within the brain are various 'control rooms', or nuclei, from which the messages (the electrical impulses and chemical 'transmitters' that pass on the impulses in the spaces between one nerve fibre and another) are co-ordinated. One of these, as mentioned in the previous chapter, is the hippocampus. There are others, less well known, that are involved, too. There's no need to go into them in detail here.

Structure of the cortex

On the surface of the brain, about half an inch thick, is the cortex, named after the bark of a tree, presumably because it's the outside layer. Within the cortex are the brain cell 'bodies' that retain the messages. From the bodies (Hercule Poirot's little grey cells) extend wire-like projections that collect and distribute messages in the form of impulses and chemical messengers to their neighbours. Pass an electrical current of the appropriate strength and frequency through the cortical cells and you will re-live the memories they have retained.

Epilepsy

This property is used in brain surgery. In some people with epilepsy, their fits are caused by an abnormality in a specific part of the cortex. There may have been an old injury with scarring at the site – people who have had head injuries in car crashes or boxers who have been knocked out several times are examples. Or there may be an abnormal blood vessel in the area, as Jane had. There may be a small tumour at the site, or the scarring may have been caused by a previous infection, such as meningitis (an inflammation of the surface coverings of the brain) or encephalitis (inflammation of the brain tissue itself).

The convulsions in such people are called 'focal'. This means that they begin with some abnormality related to the part of the brain that has been damaged. So if it's at a part of the cortex responsible for moving a finger, the fit starts with twitching of that finger. If it's at the front of the brain that deals with smell, then the fit starts with a peculiar smell. At the back of the brain, it may start with flashing lights, as the part of the brain dealing with vision is affected.

One way to deal with this type of epilepsy is to remove the scarred area – the area that is stimulating the fits. To do this the patient is asked to undergo a particular type of brain surgery that puts an electrical probe into the surface of the brain. During the surgery he or she is wide awake, the only anaesthetic used being the 'local' to 'freeze' the scalp area and the area of bone that has to be removed to expose the area in which the probe has to be used. When the probe is switched on, the patient experiences the memory relevant to the area that has been stimulated. As the probe gets closer to the focus of the fits, the patient feels close to starting a fit. That's the area that the surgeon wants to remove. When the removal is successful, the fits stop and the epilepsy is cured.

What is really interesting about this type of surgery is what the patients feel as the probe is searching for the vital area. They 'see', 'hear', and 'feel' exactly the sensations that they received perhaps years before, living through memories of a past time that has been long forgotten and would never again have been brought to mind, were it not for the surgeon's probe. This was a considerable clue to researchers about the nature of memory. The 'tape' is running for our lifetimes, and everything is there to be drawn upon if we really searched for it.

There are trillions of brain cells, and the connections between them are uncountable, so that we only use a tiny part of the brain's capacity for electrical activity and memory storage. If we tried to use it all at once, we would be overwhelmed with data. To quote a phrase from numerous science fiction films, there would be 'information overload'. It's thought that we suppress all the details we don't need to remember so that we can keep our thoughts in a reasonable order without confusion.

Mania

Mania is an illness in which the control systems do fail us. The opposite of depression, in an attack of true mania the thought processes speed up to a terrifying rate, so that a multitude of thoughts and memories flood the brain. Speech and thought are too fast for anyone listening to follow: they are described as 'raving' – from which we get the pejorative phrase 'raving mad'.

Picking and choosing memories to keep

The BBC memory programme gave a beautiful example of how we often 'shut down' our memory intake system so that we don't go into overload. The team asked volunteers to register at a hotel where they were getting together for a meeting to test their memories. As they were at the counter, a receptionist greeted them in the usual way, asking them to write down their names and addresses on the standard registration form. As they were concentrating on doing this, the receptionist ducked down underneath the counter, and a different one stood up to deal with the rest of the signing-in process. Interviewed afterwards, only a very few of the volunteers had noticed the change. Even when the swap was a woman for a man, they didn't notice. This process is so common it even has a technical name – change blindness. We are all subject to it.

Film companies take a lot of care with continuity, making sure that a scene has the same backdrop from day to day when it's taking a long time to shoot. So the actors have to wear the same clothes, and the flowers in the background have to be the same day after day. People are paid a lot to ensure that there are no hiccups. Yet they probably don't have to be so meticulous because most of us wouldn't notice the change. Of course, there are 'geeks' who spend their time trying to find the flaws in the continuity, to the extent of writing to the film companies to point out their mistakes. I wonder about them: do they spend so much time on the background that they don't take in the plot of the picture? I'd be interested to know if they can follow both the dialogue and the action and concentrate on the details at the same time.

The programme's explanation for change blindness was that the details of the receptionist were of no interest to the volunteers, so they did not register the swap for memory purposes. This must happen hundreds of times a day, as we see and hear things that do not matter, and discard them from the material we wish to keep as a memory. Do you remember the faces of the people in the bus, train or shop this morning? When we concentrate on the things we really want to remember, our brain treats them differently.

So to remember what we have just seen – for example, a receptionist's face – doesn't take place automatically. The brain decides what it wants to put into its store, and what it does not: the receptionist's face, it seems, is in the latter category. It impinges on one's brain for a few seconds, but is not transferred, via the relevant co-ordinating centre, onwards to the part of the cortex that deals with visual memory. That lies at the back of the brain, in what is called the visual cortex. Once imprinted there, it's organized into our memory circuits, along with the sound of the person's voice coming in from the auditory nerve (from the ear) to the lateral cortex. His or her smell, too, may be remembered in the frontal cortex above and behind the nose.

It follows that if you want to remember a person you have just met (a date or a new business acquaintance, but not a hotel receptionist or the thousands of people you have just passed in the street), you have to force your brain to pick up all these co-ordinated information inputs and store them in a circuit in your whole cortex, as a piece of electric circuitry.

Scans

How do we know all this? Put people into a brain scan machine and ask them to remember specific things – occasions, smells, words, music, people, places – and you will see many areas of the brain 'light up' as they do so. This was a surprise for the researchers when they began to use such tools: they had thought that a specific memory would occupy a particular area of the brain. In their terminology, they thought that memories would be more 'focal' than 'diffuse'. They now agree that many brain cells from different areas of the cortex co-operate together in forming each memory. It's small wonder that when we become brain damaged, many memories are lost.

Losing your memory – concussion and amnesia

Concussion is a good example of how memories are really lost. Hit your head hard – such as against the windscreen of a car in a crash, or against the floor of a boxing ring when you are knocked out – and you will lose your memory for the incident. Not only that, you will have amnesia (loss of memory) for several hours before it happened, and for an even longer time afterwards. As you recover, you begin to remember something of the few hours before and after the accident, but you never remember it all. Mercifully, you have lost the memory of the actual incident for good. The blow ensured that what you felt at the precise moment of the blow was never transferred to your longer-term memory banks. It may have entered your hippo-campus, but it didn't get any further.

This doesn't explain amnesia, however. The most startling form of this is the occasional case that hits the headlines – when someone is found in a street who has completely lost his memory of who he is and of his past life. In Britain throughout 2005 there was a running story of a young man found, fully dressed yet soaked to the skin as if he had just come out of the sea, who had no idea of who he was. He would not, or could not, speak, but could play the piano apparently to virtuoso standard.

In the first few weeks there were reports that he had been identified as French, Polish, Scandinavian or even Russian. Musicians asked to listen to his piano playing dispelled the idea that he had been a professional musician – his playing wasn't good enough. Eventually the media grew tired of the story, and he was left to the care of the staff of a psychiatric unit, where he gradually returned to normal. His family, from mainland Europe, identified him, and he returned to them. Little was made in the press of his return home. When he turned out to be a young man with a history of depression and a difficult psychiatric problem, the media lost interest, and he rightfully disappeared from the public eye.

Doug

This was not the case for Doug, a young American whose case was discussed in the BBC memory programme in August 2006. He was found in the New York subway, having forgotten his family, his friends and who he was. He knew nothing of his previous life, but he didn't want to know about it. He was frightened of what his memory might contain, once it returned.

His family did identify him, and they had to show him home movies and photographs to remind him of who he had been – but he still did not remember. His fear of having done something awful, or having been in some way a bad person, had been groundless. He had lived a normal life. The main feature of that life, however, was that he had been depressed. In his new life, still with no memory of the old times, his character had changed. He was, according to his friends and family, more sympathetic to others, more vulnerable, and more 'focused'. He was a more mellow and gentler person. Despite this, his sister, to whom he had been very close, still missed the old Doug, with the old personality, who could share so many memories with her.

Interestingly, although he had lost his memory, Doug still had his full grasp of language. He knew what trains and buildings and roads were, and how to get about the city. His memory loss was strictly limited to his own personal history. One part of his brain, presumably, had shut down, leaving the rest of his memory banks untouched.

What had happened to Doug? A psychoanalyst would say that Doug wanted to leave his previous life, with which he had been so dissatisfied, but that he wasn't faking his loss of memory. He has cut out of his brain every emotional experience, perhaps in an effort to survive his depression. Why this should happen suddenly on a train in Manhattan remains unanswered. It's even possible that he had suffered some trauma – perhaps a blow to the head by a potential mugger – but there was no evidence of it when he was found. For the cause of his memory loss to be a purely physical one, the blow would have to have been hard enough to damage some part of his brain involved in memory, such as his hippocampus or his temporal lobes, and this would surely have been obvious at the time.

Doug did retain certain memories from the past in a curious way. He remembered 'seeing himself' sitting on his grandmother's knee watching the moon landings. As he was only nine months old at the time and remembered looking down on himself with his grandmother, this must have been a false memory implanted later: in true memories we don't see ourselves, but look out on the world 'from ourselves', so to speak. However, he had lost his ambitions, his preferences, and his likes and dislikes. Perhaps most significantly, his father said to him, after the memory loss, that when he was a child he could shape him into what his parents wanted: now he couldn't do that. Perhaps Doug just wanted to be himself for the first time in his life.

Common to both the mystery pianist and Doug was depression. Was it possible that Doug's depression had become so bad that he was contemplating suicide – and about to use the train tracks to do so? Happily, he seems to have 'killed off' his previous personality instead, saving his life. Depression, you should remember from Chapter 1, was part of the cause of the memory lapse in the case of my gardener friend, Arthur. Emotional disturbances, especially depression, can have a profound effect on our memories. Various members of a family remember events differently, viewing them from a different standpoint, and if you are depressed at the time, the low mood may well colour the way you remember them in a different way from your siblings' memories of them. It can make the difference between a good and an unpleasant memory for the same event. When your depression lifts (as most cases do), the memories may even change for the better. There's more about this later in the book.

Distraction

It doesn't need a blow to the head, nor do we have to be depressed, to lose a memory. This morning I've been trying to do two jobs. I'm writing this book, and at the same time I have working beside me my bookkeeper, Dora Wilson, who comes in for a few hours each month to keep my records up to date. She puts me straight on my bills, expenses, invoices and taxes. She makes sure I'm organized on the business side of my writing commitments, which involve newspaper columns, books and radio programmes, as well as my medical work as a locum GP. The paperwork is huge, and best left to a professional like Dora. I would never remember it all and she is able to concentrate on it, letting me get on with what I know best.

This morning she asked me to look up the background of a cheque I had paid, and just as I was about to start rummaging in my desk for the details, the phone rang. It was my son calling about a family matter, and I had to talk for a while to him. I then sat down at my computer and got on with my previous work, having completely forgotten about the cheque.

Dora had to remind me about it, and I was suitably chastened for being a mere male who could not remember more than one task at a time! It was a good example of distraction. If you don't process a memory in the first 20 seconds, you will forget it. It will not have reached even the short-term memory 'bank' and it will be lost.

We all know about distraction. Ask children to perform a series of simple tasks, such as putting different-shaped and different-coloured building blocks in separate piles. If you let them do it immediately, they will usually perform well, even perfectly. If between making the request and them starting the task, you ask them a simple further question, such as 'When is your birthday?', they will answer the question, and forget what they had been asked to do. Diverting them from their task, no matter how briefly, makes them forget it or, more accurately, stops them from processing the memory properly. How often have you been about to do something at work when a colleague has interrupted you for a moment? And how often afterwards do you realize that you haven't done what you had set out to do?

In the next chapter we will look at how our memories develop throughout life.

4

How our memory develops –
pre-cradle to pre-grave

Babies and toddlers

From the previous chapter we learned that the first principle of having a good memory is that we build it up in an active process. Our brain makes the effort to retain the instances that are important to remember, and discards what is not needed. We have been doing this all our lives, from infancy onwards. In fact, some experts even believe it starts when we are in the womb.

They think that in the last three months of pregnancy, babies can hear sounds. Mothers-to-be who take time to rest and relax regularly to their favourite piece of music report that their babies seem to kick less and to be at rest, too, when they relax. That could be explained simply by the babies taking their 'cues' to rest from their mums: when mum is relaxing, say, listening to Mozart, there's less stress inside the womb, and the baby rests. It doesn't explain, however, what happens later, after the birth. Play the same music to a baby or toddler that's disturbed – say, agitated and crying because of some temporary discomfort – and you have a good chance of producing instant calm and a beatific smile. Try some other music, and it doesn't work. If Mozart did the trick inside the womb, then Bob Dylan won't do it afterwards. You have to put on the Mozart again.

There's also research to suggest that you can calm fretting babies up to the age of six to nine months by playing to them the noises of the womb – the rushing sounds of mum's blood-stream and her heart rhythm. In another year or so, however, playing the same sounds to the children would probably just annoy them. They lose their memories of the womb as their more mature memory processes take over.

So it seems to be well established that babies memorize sounds when they are still in the womb, which is probably important for knowing their mother's voice after they are born. However, unless their mothers have been 'reinforcing' these memories by speaking to their unborn babies regularly, by the third week after the birth they have forgotten them. It's important for mothers to speak to, and have close contact with, their babies in the first few days after they are born. Separating mum from baby immediately after birth, as used to happen in hospitals after Caesarian sections, for example, or when the baby was ill in some way, interferes with this bond, and could be more harmful than we originally thought.

I must concede here that the physiologists and anatomists who have studied the brain up to and beyond birth doubt that the infant in the womb has developed enough nerve connections to retain memories in the way that the adult can. Perhaps our auditory nerve connections, and therefore our 'hearing' memories, develop before the rest.

We think that taste, too, develops in the womb before birth. What a woman eats affects the taste of the 'amniotic' fluid in which the baby is bathed, and that enters the baby's mouth. Mothers who have a similar diet before and after the birth apparently have a better chance of success in persuading the baby to breast-feed than those who change what they eat after the birth. The baby's memory for taste determines whether or not he or she likes the breast milk.

From birth onwards we are collecting data and storing it away for use later. Parents who spend a lot of time talking to and playing with their children give them a far better memory 'storage bank' than parents who don't. The first three years are crucial: the more attention a child gets from a loving parent, one-to-one, the more likely the child is to have a good memory and to be able to use it later throughout his or her life.

Older children

However, this doesn't mean that we, as adults, can remember much that happened to us before the age of around six. Try to dredge up your earliest real, vivid memory that you can reliably depend on as being true. It's probably a fairly unusual occasion in your young life – and it probably happened at around the age of five. Perhaps it's your first day at school, or the loss of a grandparent, or something momentous in the news, like the Coronation or a royal birth.

Maybe you think you can remember something before that age, but here you are on very shaky grounds. You may instead be remembering something that your parents have told you about, and are remembering the story as if it happened directly to you. This is the false memory coming into your consciousness, much like Charles's case (see pp. 20–22). For years I had a vivid memory of what happened at the pier of our West of Scotland village at the end of the war. I remembered a German submarine surrendering to our harbourmaster, and all the young sailors lining up to be taken away in an army truck. I even remembered them giving us children some chocolates, and thinking that the Germans weren't so bad after all. I was sure I had witnessed the occasion.

Years later, trying to research it, I found that it had never happened, at least not at our pier. The scene had been in an old black-and-white film about the war that I had seen at around the age of seven, and somehow I had locked it into my memory as a personal experience. Many so-called early memories are probably in the same category. Our frontal lobes (remember that

Charles's frontal cortex had been damaged) are probably not working properly until we reach the age of seven or eight, and we cannot distinguish false from true memories until then.

The research of Dr Michelle de Hahn, at the Institute of Childhood, suggests that younger children take in less information than do adults, and they need more 'cues' to remember things. Children remember more if they are rehearsed (the lesson is repeated): it helps them to bring it back into their consciousness later. She found that how much we remember of childhood events depends a lot on how much we have been influenced by the stories told by others about them.

Older children use retrieval mechanisms to remember things better: their big memory boost is to talk about the events soon afterwards, and to concentrate on how all the senses are involved in creating the memory. If they add to what they have seen the smell, sounds and feel of an occasion, they are much more likely to remember it and to do so accurately. From the ages of seven to around fourteen, children build up excellent memories, and can recall them almost exactly with no problem – except that any two teenagers witnessing an event may well remember different things about it. It depends on how interested they are in the details. I have great memories of a trip to London to watch a football match when I was 13. I can remember almost all of the sights of London, but nothing at all about the game. My classmate remembers the game in detail, but nothing about the places we visited. He became a good footballer, I didn't. Perhaps that isn't surprising!

Puberty

After 14, puberty kicks in and emotions and sexual awakenings cloud the brain. So memories from the teenage years are erratic, to say the least. Think of your memories from, say, the age of ten, and then from the age of 16, and you will understand the difference. You can remember the words and tunes from pop music of your 16-year-old days. In fact, you probably can't, once you have brought them to mind, get rid of them again for a while. Even now, perhaps in your fifties or sixties, the songs you sing while doing the garden or driving the car are often the ones you learnt as a teenager. You will probably remember far fewer pop songs that were around after you reached the age of 25, for example. So the teenage years are a time of building up emotional memories, possibly in preference to factual ones.

This 'pop song memory' is also a good example of how learning two distinctive things about something can help you remember it better. Try to remember just the words of one of your favourite songs without the tune. Almost certainly you can't do it. You need both the tune and the words together to get it right. Once the tune is flowing in your mind, the words are there automatically. It's almost impossible to remember the words without the tune forcing itself into your consciousness.

This can lead to difficulties. Now that all students have personal stereos and headphones through which to listen to music, many can't manage without them. Teenagers who study for school and college exams and need background music all the time while they do so are at a distinct disadvantage when they enter the exam room, which is necessarily silent. They have become so conditioned to the extra sounds while thinking that they can't think properly without them. There is a view that if the music is on all the time, the student eventually doesn't hear it, and learning (which is, after all, the process of putting memories into our brains) may continue. It's proposed that if a student can hear the track change, then he or she isn't studying hard enough and the learning process will take much longer. There's some truth, too, in the argument given by students that listening to music drowns out other noises in the house. If that's so, then it may be a good thing.

What you are studying may matter where music is concerned. If it's problem solving, as in answering a maths question, then the music may not affect your sharpness. If you are trying to remember words and sentences, it's a different matter: the music is almost bound to interfere with your ability to do it. Even the type of music matters. It's easier to study to the strains of orchestral music without words than to songs in which the words play a major part.

Some experts suggest that if the music makes you happy, it may help you to remember things better. I have my doubts about this. If music had made me feel happy when I was studying, I would have switched off my studies and turned to the music. I remember to this day the roofer who constantly whistled the tune from the film *Exodus* while I was studying at medical school. The noise permeated through the whole library, and all of the students in it would gladly have murdered him! When he was asked to stop, it nearly provoked a builders' strike. It seems he was perfectly within his rights to carry on whistling, while we had to give up our right to study in silence. On the whole, and not just because of this roofer, I would favour silence when studying – the fewer distractions we have when learning, the more likely it is that the memory will stick. See the paragraph on distractions for my reasoning.

Repetitive learning

Remembering numbers and lists, such as daily tasks to do, occupy one part of your memory, but there are other memory skills that operate in a different way. Let's turn back to childhood. Education isn't just about teaching children facts – it's about training their memories too. That's why primary school teachers depended so much, for generations, on repetition. The older ones among us, and the young adults too, remember well the pain of repeating our 'times tables' and our spellings, day after day. Eventually, we got them fixed into our memories, so that 90-year-olds can still remember them.

But there is a generation of adults today who were taught differently. In the 1970s and 1980s the old rules were cast aside and children could learn in whatever way they wished. Out went spelling, grammar and numbers, and in came 'free learning'. I'm sure it was done with the best of intentions, but it left them less numerate and able to spell, and possibly even less able to communicate than their parents. And I wonder, seriously, whether their memories are as good too. The excuse is that they can use calculators for calculations and spell checks for their spelling. Spell checks have gone further in the last few years, to correct grammar as well, so that today's computer-literate adults don't need to make the effort to memorize words and numbers that their predecessors made. Remember (you read it a few pages ago, and this is, after all, a book about memory) that rule one for memory is that it's something we *do*, rather than just *is*, and it needs effort. It's an action, not a passive property of the brain, so that letting the computer take over such basic jobs may not be such a good thing.

I'm not sure that when teachers used to drill facts into children they knew that this would improve their memories, but it does seem to have worked. The basic numeracy and literacy skills that we were taught in primary schools have stayed with us far longer and more accurately than the other subjects to which we were exposed. It's not surprising to the older generation that the very young today are again being taught tables, spelling and grammar. The experiment with 'discover and learn', a teacher colleague told me, ended with children discovering that at the age of ten they had learned nothing. That's a bit extreme, but it does seem to have put that generation of children, now adults approaching middle age, at a disadvantage.

Academic learning – drilling in new facts

Perhaps the most important time for making memories is our teenage years: our last days at school and our first days approaching adulthood. As teenagers we are under two severe pressures. We have the academic pressures of having to learn huge amounts of detailed facts to pass exams. The learning by repetition that worked for our multiplication tables and spelling no longer works for the examinations leading to university entrance or to other forms of further education. We must also understand the reasoning behind the subjects we study. No one ever passed A-level physics or English simply by learning by rote. So we have to learn *how* to learn and how to put memories together in a rational and easily recallable way. That's done by revision and group discussion, and the good student soon learns that, after hearing about a new series of facts for the first time, the best way to fix them into his or her memory bank is to go over them again within a very short time – a few minutes preferably, then after an hour or two, and then, most importantly, if there is time, to review them again the next day. All of these processes fix the memories into the hippocampus and then the appropriate areas of the cortex.

At medical school, we had three lectures every afternoon. Each lasted an hour, and we students had to make notes of virtually every word. Considering that we had started each morning on the wards at around eight o'clock, talking to and taking blood samples from our little group of patients, making up our daily notes on their progress and presenting them to our respective 'chiefs' (the consultants) on the 11 o'clock ward rounds, you can imagine how tired we were when the afternoon lectures started. Then multiply the tiredness after taking notes for three hours, often on subjects at the edge of our understanding.

It wasn't uncommon for some of us to fall asleep in the lecture theatres – not a good idea, because knowing what had been said in them was crucial to our ability to pass our exams. So most of us developed a system of writing down everything our lecturers had said without bothering to try to understand it. Only later that day, after some food and perhaps a short nap, would we then turn back to the afternoon's lecture notes and try to digest them. It turned out to be an excellent way of fixing them in our memories, and to show us that we had understood more of the lecture material than we first thought. Spending an hour or two that evening was crucial. If we didn't do it, the knowledge was lost for good. It was no use just putting the notes in a folder with the intention of reading them all just before the exam. By then, the notes were indecipherable and were virtually useless.

Looking back on those days, I now realize the lectures fulfilled two functions. They not only taught us a lot of medical and surgical facts, they also taught us how to learn and how to build up a good memory, not just for our future medical practice, but also for every other facet of life. I'm sure this rule goes for every academic or technical subject. We memorize better if we are first meticulous at listening and taking notes, and then we drive the facts into our memory banks by going over them again in the short term (a few minutes or hours) and in the long term (next day).

The need for sleep

Sleep matters a lot if you want to consolidate your new memories into your brain. Many teenagers don't sleep enough, and there is a good argument for bedrooms not having televisions or computer games in them. Going to sleep in a quiet atmosphere at the correct time makes a big difference to what you have remembered from the day before. Not sleeping until after midnight and playing computer games until the early hours can lead, according to some researchers, to a drop of up to 50 points in IQ test results if they are regular habits. This may be because we use the night's sleep to transfer our newly acquired short-term memories from the hippocampus into the cortex. If we don't sleep enough, we can't accomplish all that we need to.

The quality of sleep matters too. Sleep researchers found that depriving people of rapid eye movement (REM) sleep (we go through cycles of REM and deeper sleep throughout each night) leads to a dramatic failure in memory tests, such as remembering faces and lists of words. It's during REM sleep that we dream, and when we are thought to make that all-important memory transfer from hippocampus to cortex.

Getting facts to 'stick'

The problem for teenagers is that while going through all their emotional turmoil they also have to learn masses of material for important examinations that will determine their futures. So what is the most efficient way of ensuring that the learning 'sticks' in the brain?

Today's consensus is that they should look, at the end of each day, at what they were taught that day. They should read it again the next day, then after a further week, a month, and then again after three or four months. Doing this efficiently means organizing themselves and putting time aside to do it, but it's very worthwhile. This form of study can optimize the students' opportunities and give them higher final grades than if they studied haphazardly.

So, if you are studying for exams, what is the best way to do it? Sleep matters, as it's the time you pass the new information from hippocampus to cortex, so don't 'cram' through the night. Do your studying into the evening, but stop at a reasonable time and go to sleep on it.

As for dealing with the material itself, don't try to remember a huge amount at once. Try 'chunking' – breaking the facts up into short pieces, much as you remember a telephone number. This is the way that many actors learn their scripts – a few paragraphs at a time. Some musicians do it, too, learning a few bars at a time until they are almost automatic, and only then going on to the next ones. Repeated rehearsals can drive astonishing amounts of material into a musician's memory.

Amy Johnson, Young Musician of the Year in 1984, is now an internationally renowned concert clarinet soloist. To date, her public appearances amount to over 15,000 hours. Talking on BBC Radio 4 in August 2006, she said that she had had to develop her own strategies to learn the music, including using words as cues for each passage of music. She now has more than 18 hours of music in her head that she can recall note for note at will. On one occasion when playing with the score in front of her, the pages had stuck together: her memory pulled her through without an error. Now facing her forties, she is still learning more. Yet she admits that outside music she does not have a good memory: perhaps she has to work her memory so hard for her music that she lets it 'relax' when dealing with other things. For example, she finds it difficult to remember her car number plate. It's more likely that she has a normal memory for everything else, but that it doesn't bear comparison with her amazing memory for music.

We mere mortals may feel that Miss Johnson's degree of dedication is beyond us, but we can use tricks to help us to acquire a better memory. One trick, when we need to remember lists of things, is to use mnemonics, which is a device – a short verse maybe – to aid the memory. As medical students we used them to remember the order of the twelve cranial nerves – the nerves that run directly out of the skull and not from the spinal cord.

Most of the mnemonics we used as medical students were disgusting and in bad taste, but they worked and we still remember them many years later! Astronomers are obviously much nicer people, with cleaner minds, because *New Scientist* reader Graeme Mulvaney, writing in September 2006 after the demotion of Pluto as a planet, needed a new mnemonic for the planets in the solar system.

He remembers 'My Very Excellent Mother Just Send Us Nine Pizzas' or 'Matilda Visit Every Monday, Just Staying Until Noon, Period' for the sequence of Mercury, Venus, Earth, Mars, Jupiter, Saturn, Uranus, Neptune and Pluto. I've always been confused by the sequence of the outer planets: I'm sure I won't forget them now. I'll just drop the word 'Period' from the second mnemonic.

Special days

Not all childhood memories, of course, have been drilled into us at school. Some memories are fixed into our brains for the rest of our lives because they are so shocking and made such an impression at the time. We can roll out the standard questions now – where were you when President Kennedy was shot? Or you saw the moon landings? Or you heard about the death of John Lennon or Princess Diana? Or where did you watch the tragedies of 9/11 or 7/7 unfold? Even if we think our memories are bad, we remember such occasions in considerable detail, whether we were children or adults at the time, and they stick with us for the rest of our lives. Ask people about the days before or after such dates, however, and their memories are a complete blank.

I was a house officer at the Birmingham Children's Hospital when I heard about JFK's assassination. I remember the colleague who told me about it, that I was walking into the doctor's lounge when he did so, and that we all gathered round the television to watch the developments. I don't remember anything about the patients I saw that day, or what the weather was like, but I do remember every one of the colleagues who were with me in that room. I also remember us organizing a buffet meal around the television set, rather than going to the residents' mess as usual, so that we could follow the events as they happened. But I don't remember anything about the days before or after that special one. There's a sad corollary to this tale. A few years later I heard that Geoff, my doctor friend who gave me the news about the assassination, had been shot dead in Nigeria. My memories of the JFK shooting are now inextricably linked with Geoff's violent death, too. I can't think of one without the other.

The experts suggest that for memories of disaster days like the violent deaths of famous people there is probably a particular area in the brain that retains them like no others. It can come up with a 'print-out' of the day whenever you wish. Other memories that do not touch us so personally, or that could be described as routine days, are fitted into areas of brain from which they are less easily recalled. You may even have to be helped to recall them. Plenty of people have used this knowledge to their advantage.

'Subconscious' memory

Here we are on controversial ground. Stage hypnotists are adept at 'putting people into a trance' and taking them 'back to their childhoods'. Under the 'influence', the subjects apparently live again through a particular day, say, their seventh birthday, acting as if they were children truly living through all the experiences and emotions of the time.

Sigmund Freud did the same, but for different reasons. He took his patients back in memory to their early childhood, and even in the womb, in order to find the reasons for their mental illnesses. He hoped that by doing so he could at last explain their behaviour, and perhaps even cure them. It became the basis of psychoanalysis. The psychoanalyst Carl Jung went further. He proposed that there were 'inherited memories' deep in everyone's subconscious, passed down from our ancestors.

Neither of these techniques rings true. If you volunteer for stage hypnosis you are probably of a particular mindset in the first place, either being willing to be 'put under' or wanting to show off in front of your companions. The hypnotist uses simple tests to weed out the truly susceptible from the cynics, and sends back to their seats the people who won't respond as he plans. Then he can concentrate on the 'susceptibles'. They do exactly as he orders them to and behave appropriately when asked to remember things because they want to make a show of it. There is probably no relationship between their actual seventh birthday, for example, and the one they act out on the stage.

The Freud and Jung camps were probably doing something similar with most of their patients. If you are lying on a couch being asked to 'open out' to a great and respected psychoanalyst, you will provide a story, no matter how bizarre it might be. That goes, too, for stories of reincarnation. There are dozens of people today who claim they have memories of being Cleopatra or Napoleon. Very few remember more everyday lives, such as being a farm labourer or a Victorian factory worker. There's a particular problem with Jung, who believed that memories could be inherited and that memories of experiences of previous lives were passed on along with the genes during reproduction. That doesn't explain the memories of previous deaths, say, on the battlefield (a common memory for those who recall being heroic soldiers) because obviously the reproduction and therefore the inheritance of memories took place long before the death.

So we must be wary of memories forced out of us by other people, even in circumstances that are respectably clinical, as on the psychiatrist's couch. Psychoanalysis has diminished as an orthodox medical treatment in the last 20 years or so as it has become clear that dragging out possibly false memories from people with emotional and psychiatric disturbances can do more harm than good. It's sometimes better to leave bad memories undisturbed than to bring them out into the open. That's especially true if the memories are not entirely factual and have been distorted with the passage of time and the influence of other people.

If you feel that your memory is deteriorating with age, the message to take from this section on 'subconscious' memories is not to dabble in it as it may do you harm. By all means try to improve your memory, but doing so by lying on a couch or sitting in a chair and letting some professional drag it out of you is probably counterproductive. There are much better ways of improving your memory, which we will go into in more detail later.

Improving your memory at any age

Although this chapter has been devoted largely to how we develop our memories in childhood, it's highly relevant to us in our later lives, through middle age and beyond. We (relatively) 'oldies' had to try hard to hone our memory skills as students, and they are a useful basis for improving our memories at any age. Our memories should work as well in later life as when we were younger, provided we know how to use them. It's our changing lifestyles as we age that get in the way of remembering things, rather than the ageing process itself. To start with, we no longer have the pressure on us to amass all those facts that are imposed on us by the educational system, so we just don't bother trying.

Yet all this stuff about children and teenagers is wholly relevant to the adult brain – the one you and I are worrying about, because it's beginning to age. The processes by which we remember things are just the same, regardless of whether we are

16 or 60. We don't suddenly start to deteriorate when we reach 40 or even 60 or, for that matter, 80. If we are generally healthy we retain our abilities to form new memories and to retain and recall old memories. It's just that with age, we don't force ourselves to do so. Young adults building up lives for themselves have to work hard on their memory skills to get on. We older folk have lost that impetus and drive, and tend not to bother so much. If there is one universal rule in biology, it's 'if you don't use it, you lose it'.

5

Some special aspects of memory – faces, names and places

Remembering faces ...

Angela

At the age of 40, Angela caught a severe viral infection of the brain – encephalitis – and fell ill suddenly. Her first symptom was a severe headache, and she quickly lost consciousness, not waking up from her coma for six weeks. When she did so, she didn't recognize her husband or children. Their faces were frightening to her, and so was her own, because she thought she was back in her twenties.

Over the four years since then, she and her family have had to try to rebuild all her memories, but she seems to have lost for ever her ability to recognize people's faces. She has to concentrate on a particular aspect of a person's appearance and link it to what she has learned about that individual's past and the circumstances in which they met. It still hurts when she meets someone in the street and does not recognize her, only to find that she is her sister, or even her daughter.

This loss of ability to recognize a face is almost impossible to help because there is no short-cut or easy way to improve it. Angela has been told to construct a 'friendship book' in which she lists all the things she knows about each person. It's more than just an address book. Obviously the address is important, but also in the book are people's likes and dislikes, where Angela met them, in what circumstances, what they do, where they go for holidays, and any small unusual thing that might stick in Angela's memory that can be fitted to the face. It's very difficult, but Angela is slowly improving.

She spends hours studying photographs of friends and famous people whom she might be expected to know, to test herself every day on face recognition, and to try to train herself to recognize friends' faces when she meets them. However, it's a slow process. In the meantime she uses the friendship book's information to help her. For example, one friend has red hair, another has a limp, yet another wears a particular design of earrings: she can remember all these characteristics and then put a name to them. But if her first friend is wearing a hat, and the second is sitting down, and the third has obscured her ears with a new hair-do, she doesn't recognize them. She may not even recognize her son when he is on the football team: she has to remember the number on the back of his shirt to make sure she is cheering on the right boy.

Angela's inability to remember people's faces is extreme, and is the consequence of her infection-induced brain damage. The area of cortex that she used to use to recognize faces has gone for good, courtesy of the virus. Nevertheless, most of us, without such a serious insult to our brains, if we were honest, would admit to some difficulty in remembering faces. It can work both ways. We fail to recognize a face we should know from past meetings, and sometimes we think we have recognized someone when in fact he or she is a complete stranger.

This sort of memory difficulty is not a sign of memory weakness, nor is it a portent of impending doom, leading to dementia and misery. It's just what happens when we don't pay close attention to a face when we see it for the first time. It's normal, and nothing to worry about. We see millions of faces in our lifetime, and it would be senseless and cause difficulties if we tried to remember them all. Of course we recognize a face that we see all the time, like a member of our close family, or a neighbour or friend, or someone famous on television. But casual acquaintances, or someone we met years ago, and not since? That would be a struggle for anyone, and remains so. It happens to get worse as we grow older because we have met so many more people than we did when we were younger.

The real problem is that there isn't much that we can do about it, except to do as Angela does and practise face memory tests on lots of photographs, many times a week. That isn't practical for normal living. We *can* improve, though, and one way to do it is, when we meet someone new, to make a mental note of something different about the face or the person at the time of the meeting, and try to put it into our memory again a few minutes later. Link the note with the name and, if relevant, what the person does for a living and some detail about the occasion you met. For example, was it on holiday and, if so, where, and what were the circumstances? The combination of the general look of the face, some individual characteristic of it, along with the context of the meeting and the person's name, all together in one part of your memory, should reinforce your memory of the face next time you meet.

Remembering names ...

Names are a real problem, and probably the most difficult to remember, especially if you haven't seen the person for a while. The problem with names is similar to that of random numbers – they mean nothing on their own, so they are easily forgotten soon after you hear them. When you have to learn new names, particularly of people, try to link them with the context of the meeting: where, when and any other aspect of it that might stick in your mind.

The difficulty with names, too, is that the ability to remember them does truly deteriorate with age. In your forties you probably have no trouble with names of politicians, or footballers, or media personalities, or actors. By the time you are in your sixties one of the main worries you have is bringing to mind the name of a newsreader that you see every night on television. This scares you, because you think it's one of the first signs of dementia. *Surely* you can recall his or her name, you think, but it has completely escaped you. You try time and again, but fail. Then, hours later, suddenly the name springs to mind.

You haven't forgotten the name, you just haven't been able to recall it from your memory store. It was there all the time. We are not sure why this happens, but it seems to be universal, and is part of growing older, without being abnormal in the sense of it being the beginning of disease.

Trying to improve our ability to remember names is a bit easier than improving memory for faces. But as with all aspects of memory training, we have to work at it. As with numbers, it's a good idea to give each name a meaning. Teachers who have to learn new names in the classes they take every year have told me of tricks they use. They are not infallible, but they do help a lot until the children have been in the classroom for so long that they have become as familiar as family.

One problem with names is that the first name doesn't have any obvious connection with the second, so you have to combine your 'image' of the first name with that of the second. A good friend of mine, a teacher, has a system for first names that includes set 'pictures' in his mind of people in history. So for anyone called Henry he remembers that famous Holbein picture of Henry VIII. For John, he remembers John the Baptist's head on a plate. For Thomas, there's Thomas the Tank Engine, and for Harold, there's a medieval crowned head with an arrow in the eye. For girls, Elizabeth conjures up a picture of the first Elizabeth on her white charger, reviewing her troops, and for Mary, obviously, her counterpart of the Scots. Again he sees her severed head, which might say something about his character that I wouldn't like to delve into too deeply! He is English, after all, and a history teacher! As a Scot, I might be excused for using different images.

He attaches historical 'pictures' to most women's names, but you could use film or television stars or sportswomen instead, anyone whose first name might stick in your mind, depending on your interests. For me, the name Julie reminds me of Julie London and her song 'Cry me a river' – that shows my age. Perhaps more up to date, when introduced to a Rose, I file her away with an image of Hyacinth Bouquet's feckless man-devouring sister from ... now what's that series called again?

Yes, I've got it – *Keeping Up Appearances*. More garden-oriented people might use a real rose instead.

Once you have the first name, you then need to combine it with the second. Many names are easy: like Smith, Baker, Porter, Carpenter, Farmer and so on. Fit the first image with what their names suggest they do, and you'll find them easy to recall. Henry VIII putting dough into an oven, and you get the idea. King John signing the Magna Carta is another. Harold with the arrow in his eye has been one of mine for a few years, but I now can't get a certain Dr Shipman out of my mind when I'm introduced to a new Harold. Not very nice, really, but whenever you see the face again, that image will float in front of you.

It's not so easy when the names aren't occupation-linked. For me, Wilson dredges up images of dear old Harold and his pipe, writing out his surprising resignation. Brown reminds me of the song about making my brown eyes blue; Campbell conjures up a tin of soup; and Macdonald, a beefburger (if I want to succeed in selling this book to Scots at home or abroad, I'd better mention both clans equally). For more complex names, like Warburton, I think of a battle in which everyone wears a certain type of two-piece suit. For Bill Warburton, there is an army of people wearing such suits and ready for action, with weapons, presenting me with a huge invoice for them. Charles Seagrave suggests our dear Prince of Wales sliding off a plank from a ship.

So it goes on. It seems unnecessarily complicated, but once you are used to it, it takes a remarkably short time to put into practice. You will find it fun, and soon it becomes a routine that you can do automatically and in a very short time whenever you meet someone new. Try it on some well-known friends' names and you will get the gist of it. You will make up your own list, of course, depending on your main interests. Teachers who use these techniques find they remember a whole classroom of names within a few days.

Names and 'old-timers'

You think you are too old to be able to do this? Then you should listen to Baroness Betty Boothroyd, probably the most popular and most well-known Speaker of the House of Commons ever, about her methods of remembering names. How did she remember the names of the 650 members of the House when she became Speaker, at an age beyond which quite a few of us have retired? She spoke about it in that BBC memory programme in August 2006, when she was 76 years young – and still working hard in the House of Lords. She is absolute proof that you can still have a good memory well into your eighth decade.

She made up an A–Z book of members with their names and photographs, and tried to fix them into her memory alphabetically. She also invited all the new members to her rooms for welcome drinks, in batches of 25 or so, so that she could meet them all personally. She asked them to find a seat in the House that they felt was right for them, and always, if possible, to sit in it, so that she could relate the name and face with the place in which they sat. And she had a personal civil servant to whisper names into her ear when she needed the extra information.

Now, she says, she finds it difficult to remember the names of people she has known for years. She has to set priorities every day and make lists before going shopping. But there are numbers from her childhood that she still remembers – and I was delighted to hear that she and I have something in common. We both were sent as children to collect 'messages' (the North Country and Scottish word for shopping) by our mothers and grandmothers, and we still remember the family Co-op dividend number. If you are reading this, your ladyship, ours was 3434! I must have last used it when I was eight years old.

Murray Walker told of his memory on the same programme. He was the voice of Formula 1 racing for more years than I could count, and continued well into his seventies. At the age of 82, in 2006, his wife says he still has a brilliant memory, but only for anything with an engine in it. Avid listeners will remember the ease with which the information rolled off his tongue with every race. He was famous for his gaffes in English – we all remember his 'Unless I'm very much mistaken' – but he rarely made an error of fact. Before each race he stuck a card with all the facts he needed on his monitor. He made himself write them all down because it 'consolidated his memory'. Once that was done, he probably used it only as a fail-safe, once or twice a race.

Remembering places, with directions ...

Memories for places and how to get to them are different again. We may have a fabulous memory for faces, but none at all for directions. Let's go back to the London cabbies. They start off with no better a memory for directions than anyone else, yet after a year or two they seem to have a complete atlas in their heads.

They apparently divide into two camps. Some try to visualize the map of London in their heads. There are the main arterial roads, down which they travel most to get from one part of the city to another. Then there are the subsidiary roads, into which they turn to get into a complex of minor, residential roads. And finally there are the small streets with the addresses to which the clients have to be delivered. Many cabbies learn them in that order: first fixing the larger roads, then the middle-sized ones, then the smallest roads. Doing that, they gradually build up the 'map' in their memory banks until they get it right. They spend hours and hours on it, in constant repetition, until they are almost photograph-perfect. They know the names of the streets automatically.

But there is another way. Some cabbies build up their knowledge from landmark buildings at the corners of crossroads, then take their cues from them. They visualize London not as a map, but as a series of easily recognizable buildings – a restaurant, a church, a pub, a town hall, a station – anything that stands out and that they can use as a marker for the next stage of a journey. I remember bus journeys to my school, when the conductors would call out each stop as they came to them. They divided up into three types. There were those who called out the street names, others who went by the churches nearby, and others who preferred to use the local pubs. So a stop could either be Bryant Road, St Peter's or the Dog and Duck, depending on the conductor's preference.

However you wish to remember directions depends on the type of memory system that you prefer. You may feel more comfortable with the map or the landmarks: they seem equally efficient. Returning to that BBC radio programme, two groups of people were faced with the Hampton Court Maze. One lot was shown a map of the maze beforehand, and asked to memorize it. The other was told that at each corner there was a symbol or word, and that each one meant that they were to turn in a particular direction. They were asked to memorize the direction given by each symbol in turn, then they were let loose in the maze. Both groups got lost, and there was no real advantage of one system over the other. It was clear, however, that the self-appointed leaders of the groups were no better than the 'followers' at remembering the instructions or the map.

If you aren't much use at remembering directions, there's no easy way of improving this skill. As with all types of memory, you just have to work at it. Repetition is still the basis of making it better. If you are going on a journey, write down the directions so you have them in the car with you, but go over them the day before once or twice and then immediately before you get in the car. And decide on your system – the map or the landmarks, or even a combination of the two. The more you reinforce the memory, the better you will be at your navigation.

Day-to-day memory – say, for shopping

Having read so far, you will already be beginning to train your memory-gathering and recall skills.

Imagine you are ready to go shopping, and you have drummed into your brain a list of foods and domestic materials you need. You are confident that you will remember them when you arrive at the supermarket. But when you get there, you realize that not only have you forgotten to pick up the list when you left the house, you have forgotten most of the items on it. You wander around the aisles, trying desperately to visualize the list, but when you return home, you find that your memory has been woefully inadequate. So you need another trip to the shops to make up the difference between what you actually remembered and what was on the original list.

Sounds familiar? Of course it does. We have all done it. We try that children's game – I went to market, and I bought ... Remember it? The children sit around in a ring and the first gets one item to remember, the next adds one, the third another, and so on until there are perhaps eight items on the list that must be remembered in order without forgetting one. Few children manage to reach nine.

The problem with the game is that the items are all discon-nected, so without connecting them to a 'story' it's virtually impossible to remember them beyond that magical number of seven. If you can make up a story around them, it's a different matter.

This is where the 'Roman room' system comes in. The original idea was that you were to imagine a typical Roman villa with a large main room, inside which are seats, a sofa, perhaps an oil lamp or two, some ornaments, say a bust or vases, a painting or two, a fireplace, and doors to the outside, where there is a garden with trees, perhaps a pond, and flowerbeds, with a wall around it. In the wall is a gateway, through which you can reach the road outside, on which you can walk, or take your chariot to the forum, where you can shop to your heart's delight.

Sounds odd? It gets odder! Now that you have fixed this scene into your mind, you are going to connect your shopping items to the fittings and furniture in the room, the objects in the garden outside, perhaps a creeper on the wall, and the road outside it. So, in your mind, you place, say, the bacon on the table, the milk by a vase, the bread on a chair, the tea by a picture, and so on, putting one of your shopping items beside or on one of the objects you have so diligently imagined in your particular Roman room. Thoroughly go through which objects you have linked to which items of shopping in your mind before leaving for the supermarket, and remind yourself of where they are on the way. Can you remember them when you get there? You may be staggered by how accurate you will be.

The 'Roman room' system can be easily adapted to your own system. Picture the inside of your own house and the garden and street outside, and 'put' each of your shopping items against one of them. You can make the process into a walk. You get up out of your favourite chair (the tea), walk across the carpet (the bread is on the floor), and open the door (the milk is hanging by a plastic bag on the handle). In the hall the tinned fruit is on the table, and the meat is on the mat. Through the door, on the step there are your eggs. Walk past the border along the path to the front gate, and the washing-up liquid is nestling at the roots of the rose bush. On the gatepost is that bottle of wine that you will treat yourself to when you realize how good your memory has become.

You can make the walk as long as you like. I have a friend who lives in a seaside fishing village. A retired widower, in his eighties, he was worried that his poor memory might be the thing that eventually would lead to him having to go into a residential care home. He has to walk about a quarter of a mile from his home near the harbour to the shops in the main street.

He starts his 'Roman room' walk by imagining he is on one of the fishing boats coming into the harbour, and puts some of his shopping on the deck, among the nets and in the wheelhouse. The next items are on the harbour wall and by the lifebelt hanging there. Then comes the lifeboat station, the cottages along the front, and his own house and garden. By this time, he has all of his weekend needs fulfilled. He thinks of them on the way to the shop once or twice, and he remembers them perfectly when he has arrived.

All you have to do is to construct the architecture of the mental 'walk' for routine use, and you will find that you can hold much more in your memory banks than you thought you could. With practice, you can hold 20 or more items in your head without much trouble or strain – but it's still advisable to take your list with you as well. Just to check, of course.

6

Just how good is your memory?

Measuring memory – the digit span test

We have been measuring children's memories for over a century. Victorian educationists were using the 'digit span test' from the 1880s onwards to measure memory. They also thought it measured intelligence as well, and it formed part of the old IQ (Intelligence Quotient) tests that they and several generations of their successors used to separate children at the age of 11 via the 11-plus exam. They would be surprised to learn today that we differentiate between tests of memory and of intelligence: the two are not closely related. Many of us do badly in one and well in the other. In a class of eight-year-olds of equal intellect, some of the children will have less than half of the memory capacity of those with the best memory skills. They don't do so well academically later, unless their teachers can help them to improve. One way to do that is to help them deal with distractions – a main cause of their poor memory at that age. As adults, too, we can train our memories to be better. It's more difficult with true tests of intelligence.

The digit span test is simply a series of seven random numbers that you are asked to remember in sequence. You can be asked to repeat the sequence immediately, then after a few minutes, and then perhaps half an hour or so later, after being distracted by other tasks. You may be asked to repeat them in reverse order, and you may also be asked to try to remember more than seven numbers – probably up to nine.

Most people with a normal memory and no training can remember seven numbers in the digit span test. It's an interesting total because it isn't exclusive to human memory. Animal trainers say that they can get performing birds, usually of the crow family, such as rooks or jackdaws, to remember up to seven objects, but almost never more than that. Remembering nine seems to be impossible for birds, and much more difficult for children and adults.

The problem with random numbers is that they mean nothing in isolation. Yet we can remember phone numbers – a series of ten or more numbers – because we break them down into 'chunks'. We remember the 5-digit district code, because it usually starts with 01 and is followed by three numbers that are easy to keep in our heads because we use them a lot. Then there is the local area code, another three numbers with which we are familiar, and reasonably easy to remember. Finally there is the three-digit personal number, which may be the most difficult to recall. Yet if it's a number we ring often we can usually rattle it off without bother. What we are remembering are three series of three or four numbers joined together. Seven random numbers that mean nothing and that we have never heard before are a different matter.

Yet give Dominic O'Brien, eight times World Memory champion (yes, there is such a person), a series of 20 random numbers to remember and he will rattle them off, not just immediately, but half an hour later, and even the next day. You can't do that by simply breaking them down into chunks – the only way to remember them is to add meaning to them, so that you are telling yourself a story that includes the numbers in some easy-to-recall way. To give a simple example:

Try remembering 21396610225765458499.

You can make up your own story about it, but here is a sample. You are given the key of the door because it's your 21st birthday. Through the door there's Richard Hannay (the hero of John Buchan's novel) at the bottom of a staircase with 39 steps. You walk up it with him and at the top is William the Conqueror (1066, hence the 66). (You might try the England World Cup success (1966), but I'm a Scot!) William is taking you to see the Prime Minister at number 10 Downing Street, where you feast on two swans for dinner (the number 2 looks like a swan) and a tin of baked beans (Heinz 57). You hear that the Prime Minister is retiring (he's 65) and his last job is to commemorate the end of the Second World War (45). He says his main aim has been to avoid an Orwellian totalitarian state (1984) and he offers you an ice-cream cone with a chocolate bar stuck in it as a farewell present (99).

Sounds ridiculous? First try to remember the numbers as they are *without* the story. Then get the story into your head and try to remember the numbers again. After you have put this book down and gone away to busy yourself with something else, try to remember the numbers again. You will be amazed.

World Memory champions use exactly these tricks to remember long series of numbers, and do it astonishingly quickly. According to the *Lancet*, 19 August 2006, the current world record for memorizing correctly the order of a shuffled pack of playing cards is 31.03 seconds. People like Dominic O'Brien can commit to memory hundreds of random numbers and repeat them forwards and backwards at will.

Obviously, there is no need to hone your memory skills to a level anywhere near that of Dominic, but you can use a much scaled-down version of his 'tricks' to improve this particular type of memory skill for your everyday life.

The Mini Mental State Examination (MMSE)

Of course, memory isn't just about numbers: it encompasses all the other facets of memory described in the previous chapters. In 1975, Dr M. F. Folstein and colleagues published a paper called 'Mini-Mental State: A Practical Method for Grading

Question	Score
What is the day of the week?	1
What is the month?	1
What is the date?	1
What season is it?	1
What year is it?	1
What city/town are we in?	1
What county?	1
What country?	1
What building are we in?	1
What floor are we on?	1
Repeat after me 'ball car man' (don't score this question)	
Repeat again 'ball car man' (score after this second trial)	3
Spell the word WORLD (don't score)	
Now try to spell it backwards (DLROW)	5
What were the three words you were asked to repeat (ball car man)?	3
What is this called (show a watch)?	1
What is this called (show a pencil)?	1
Repeat after me 'no ifs and buts'	1
Read and do what is written down (card states 'close your eyes')	1
Write a short sentence	1
Copy this drawing (two interlocking pentagons)	1
Take this paper in your left hand (or right if the person is left-handed)	1
Fold it in half	1
Put it on the floor	1
Total Score	**30**

the Cognitive State of Patients for the Clinician' (*Journal of Psychiatric Research*, volume 12, pp. 189–98).

The test, now known as MMSE, is still used, more than thirty years later, by GPs to assess memory as a standard whenever there is doubt that a poor memory might signal a more serious underlying condition. To take it, you sit comfortably and are asked what may seem simple questions by a tester, who notes down the answers. It's like a normal conversation with someone dressed like you are – no white coats or instruments to intimidate you. Each answer is allocated a number, and the total should be 30. A score of 26 or more is considered normal: below that we start to suspect a serious memory loss linked perhaps to Alzheimer's disease.

You can try it yourself; see page 64.

The MMSE was designed to detect changes in your reasoning powers, your sense of time and place, memory, attention, understanding, naming ability, and practical skills. It's obviously very basic, but if you found it particularly easy and scored 28 to 30, you can reassure yourself that although your memory is bad, you are very unlikely to have Alzheimer's – and that, after all, is probably your main worry. A score of 27 or below, however, should make you consider a visit to your doctor, who will want to do more detailed tests to try to confirm or rule out that your memory problems may be linked to early dementia. I won't go into these tests further here, as this book isn't about Alzheimer's disease. (If you would like to know more, please read *Living with Alzheimer's Disease*, also published by Sheldon Press, in which these tests are described and in which the association of memory loss with intellectual loss is discussed at length.)

The MMSE was not originally intended to make definite diagnoses of dementia, and it would still not be used in isolation to do so. Its purpose was simply to provide researchers with a group of people with early dementia (who score between 10 and 25 on MMSE) who could be included in clinical trials of new treatments for dementia. They were chosen because they might be expected to respond in such a way that a changing score could be assessed statistically. People with scores of 26 and above would have little room for an improvement that could become statistically significant, and people with scores under 10 would have such severe dementia that drugs would not be expected to work for them.

My purpose in including the test here was partly to reassure you (because if you are reading this book, you are likely to score highly on MMSE) that your memory loss is almost certainly not due to Alzheimer's or any other form of dementia. You almost certainly know the limits to your memory and are keen to widen them: this is not a sign of dementia.

If your doctor does feel you have significant memory loss that needs treatment, the next step may be for you to be enrolled in your local memory clinic. The next chapter describes the work of our local clinic in Dumfries and Galloway, in south-west Scotland.

On the other hand, your doctor may feel, after the consultation, that your memory loss indicates an underlying illness. If that is the case, it has to be ruled out or confirmed so that you can have the appropriate treatment. A common cause of memory loss, for example, is an underactive thyroid gland; another is depression. Circulation problems can lead to memory difficulties, as can something as simple as a vitamin deficiency. Chapters 8 to 10 describe how we deal with them.

7

Memory loss clinics

I live and work in south-west Scotland, a region blessed with beautiful scenery, a good quality of life and, above all, excellent health and medical services. It has been my good fortune to be able to work there for most of my life as a GP. Relationships between family doctors, consultants and all the other health services in hospital and in the community have been unparalleled. This is especially true of the services for patients with memory loss, so I've written this chapter for the people who run our memory loss clinics. Most of it is based on a conversation I had with Catherine, one such memory clinic link worker.

Catherine has a background in social services, and her role in the memory clinic is to advise people on such things as their finances, their benefits, aids to help their memories, and on other means of support provided locally. These include 'taxi cards' for people who can no longer drive, which pay for up to a third of their transport needs, and advice on when and how to give power of attorney to relatives. She co-ordinates the assessments of memory loss, investigations such as scans, treatments and drugs if necessary, and works alongside GPs, clinic doctors, specialist nurses, occupational therapists and social workers.

She visits people in their homes, initially fortnightly, then monthly, and every three to six months to follow their progress. Once a year each patient visits the clinic for a consultant review. The clinic currently has around 2,000 people on its books (from a population of around 400,000) and enrols around 150 new patients each year. Last January Catherine was able to discharge

78 patients from the clinic's books because they had improved so much that their regular GP could follow them up.

People are referred to the clinic by their family doctors. In our area it's a simple process: the referral is sent electronically at the time of the GP consultation, bypassing the wait for letters, and ensuring the fastest possible reply. If you are referred, your first contact with the clinic staff is with the nurse, who talks to the family, makes an initial assessment, and discusses the ramifications of memory loss in a quiet and competent way in the best place to do it – your home.

In this initial visit, one aim is to get you (and, if necessary, your family) to understand what is happening to your ability to maintain a good memory. If you are angry, frustrated, even agitated, about your memory difficulties, it goes a long way to easing the stresses you feel – and that in itself can help to improve your memory and your thought processes.

The practical help, too, is important. For example, on that first visit you will be introduced to the idea that memory is an active process that you need to nurture. Your memory 'adviser', perhaps a nurse, or someone like Catherine, will introduce you to all sorts of ways of improving your memory. They include diaries to fill in each day, notepads to write everything down about the day's events, to having daily papers delivered so that you are always reminded of the date and the day of the week, and can keep up to date with current events. They are also a good source of brain-exercising crosswords and puzzles such as Sudoku. Television's Ceefax and Teletext also provide information and interest, and there are internet sites that will hold your interest. All these are encouraged by the memory clinic staff, and serve to keep the brain occupied.

Catherine's group sets goals to be achieved every week. They start by asking you to meet friends more often, say for morning coffee, for which you have to plan ahead, exercising your memory to do so, and during which you will be stimulated socially as well as mentally. Meeting friends and family, and being outgoing, rather than inward-looking, she says, can be a big help in retaining your memory and even improving it.

She is constantly surprised and encouraged by the success of these simple steps for all kinds of memory loss, even when it's associated with early dementia, as in Alzheimer's disease. She is also encouraged by her experience of medical treatment of memory loss, which she admits is not her field, but with which she has witnessed considerable memory enhancement. The cholinesterase inhibitor treatments for Alzheimer's disease (for which, see next page), she says, have worked in people with pure memory loss and no discernible dementia. She has also seen good results with ginkgo biloba, and with high doses of Vitamin E, although this is a personal view and not the result of controlled clinical trials.

Often, for example, memory loss means that driving can become a nightmare. This is where the taxi cards are a godsend. Our taxi cards cost £3 for three years, and patients whose memory problems are so bad that they can't drive find them invaluable. The taxi firms are registered with the local council, and users can receive up to one-third of their taxi journeys free. All bus journeys for pensioners are free – the passes being valid throughout Scotland.

I was fascinated to hear from Catherine that early Alzheimer's disease, which often starts with memory loss, does not necessarily mean that you must stop driving. It does mean that a report of the diagnosis must be sent to the Driver and Vehicle Licensing Agency (DVLA) in Cardiff, and that your licence should be reviewed once a year. But many people for whom driving is an essential part of their lives can continue to drive locally, where they are totally familiar with the roads. Catherine knows of one 57-year-old with considerable memory loss who can still drive and continue his work, provided he has all his memory aids with him.

About two-thirds of the people in the clinic have Alzheimer's disease. Memory loss is a feature of Alzheimer's, and there are tests to distinguish memory problems on their own from the more far-reaching consequences of Alzheimer's and other forms of dementia – which means loss of intellect. Catherine has found that the clinic is as beneficial for people with dementia in helping their memories as for people without it.

Other causes of memory loss among her clinic patients include multiple small strokes (or 'multi-infarct' disease), old head injuries, and heart conditions such as abnormal rhythms ('arrhythmias') in which the blood flow to the brain is sometimes inadequate. These conditions are covered in the following chapters.

As a GP, and as mentioned at the end of the last chapter, I must add two other illnesses of older age that tend to cloud the memory – an underactive thyroid and depression. People with memory loss linked to these conditions don't reach the memory clinic, because treatment for their underlying illnesses should be enough to improve their memories. I've allotted a chapter to each.

Objections to memory clinics

Personally I wholeheartedly support memory clinics such as the ones in our region that are staffed by professionals such as Catherine, but I must add that some consultants in psychiatry disagree with them. Writing in the *British Medical Journal* on 2 September 2006 (volume 333, pp. 491–3), Drs Anthony Pelosi, Seamus McNulty and Graham Jackson suggested that they are 'diverting resources from high quality integrated care'.

Frankly, I was shocked by their conclusions, but I feel I must present their views here if the book is not to be seen as biased. They agree that memory clinics were useful when their main function was to improve recruitment of patients for research into the causes of dementia and memory loss and for controlled trials of new drugs. However, they saw them as less useful when more memory clinics were established after the introduction of drugs to treat dementia and memory problems. They saw the spread of such clinics, employing large teams of people with different disciplines and expertise, as a waste of much-needed NHS resources. Some of the clinics, they wrote, are funded by the manufacturers of the drugs being used in Alzheimer's disease, and this was unacceptable to them.

Their objections to widespread memory clinics fall into several categories. One is that the patients, at their first visit, undergo intense assessments of their nervous systems, even though what is found then rarely makes a difference to their ultimate treatment. A consultant evaluates every new patient, identifying such problems as circulation disorders, drug side-effects (sometimes another cause of memory loss), and vitamin deficiencies (due to poor diet or difficulties in feeding properly). This, Dr Pelosi and his colleagues suggest, is part of the day-to-day work of psychiatrists who specialize in old age, and who only need to refer their patients to other specialists when they are really needed.

Dr Pelosi's group also criticize memory clinics because the nurses 'spend their time monitoring the decline of patients taking cholinesterase inhibitors [drugs to improve mental ability in Alzheimer's disease] rather than ensuring the delivery of multidisciplinary care plans'. For 'multidisciplinary', read 'the co-ordination of nursing, social, occupational and medical care'. This criticism cannot be levelled at the memory clinic in my area.

A further criticism put forward by the *British Medical Journal* article is that specialist memory clinics do not offer care in the community to their patients as they decline: they confine themselves to the easy parts of the management of dementia. They leave, it claims, the difficult part to 'ordinary' old age psychiatry teams, who have to arrange what the article calls 'proper' management, and who are under pressure already from their workloads. Their task is not made easier, it is proposed, when potential members of the old-age teams have been recruited to memory clinics.

Where do I stand on memory clinics as a whole? I feel that our clinic in south-west Scotland is useful and practical, and helps many people for whom there are few other options. It takes a considerable load from the shoulders of their family doctors (something I naturally appreciate) and I see it as complementary to, rather than draining or putting pressure upon, the other psychiatric services. I hope our local psychiatrists feel the same. I will continue to refer patients to memory clinics for assessment and treatment.

8

Your thyroid and your memory

The thyroid gland lies in the front of your neck, around the lower edge of your larynx, or Adam's apple. Its purpose is to produce two hormones, thyroxine (usually referred to as T4) and tri-iodothyronine (T3). They work together to control the speed at which each cell in our bodies 'conducts its business'. With normal levels of the two thyroid hormones circulating in our bloodstreams, everything ticks along as it should:

- The fat cells release just enough fat when asked to do so.
- The muscle cells, including those in the heart, contract at the right speed and with the right force.
- The brain cells pass on their messages at the normal rate and in the usual number.
- The liver cells control the amount of glucose released into the bloodstream so that it remains in the normal range.
- The digestive cells in the gut and the muscle co-ordination in the bowel combine so that digestion and excretion carry on as normal.
- In fact, all the body's systems function just at the pace they are designed to.

It follows that if your thyroid gland starts to fail, all these systems slow down. The heart beats more slowly, your brain works more slowly, your body's metabolism slows, so that you put on weight, you become constipated, and you become generally duller in your responses. You think more slowly than before and, with that mental sluggishness, your memory begins to flag too.

When the thyroid starts to fail, you often don't notice this yourself. Although you are not as bright or as energetic as you were, it's often up to other people to recognize what is happening. The process doesn't cause you any pain, and you don't realize that you have changed. Often it's only when someone close to you starts to worry that you are not the person you were that you are taken to the doctor.

Two typical underactive thyroid patients come immediately to mind:

Belle

Belle was 73, a widow who lived on her own in the terraced house she had shared with her husband for 50 years. He had died a year before, and she had become something of a recluse. Her neighbours were kindly, and thought that her keeping herself to herself was simply part of her grief, but they looked in on her once or twice a week to keep contact.

Recently, though, they found that she was forgetting things. She hadn't put the bins out on time, and she wasn't as sharp as before when chatting to them. She didn't seem to be keeping up with the news as she used to, and she sometimes wasn't sure what day it was. They also noticed that she was losing her hair, and she had aged, her face becoming coarser, her eyes duller, and she had put on a stone or two in weight.

Oddly, she felt cold even on warm summer days. When everyone else was in summer dresses, she had on her winter coat, and complained that she was never warm.

Happily, her neighbours were so worried about her that they told the district nurse, who visited her and almost immediately thought of a thyroid problem. She realized that Belle had all the signs and symptoms of an underactive thyroid, and was quite shocked by the change in her appearance.

Belle fitted almost exactly the first description of a woman with thyroid disease, written by Dr W. W. Gill in 1874 ('On a cretinoid state supervening in adult life in women', in *Transactions of the Clinical Society*, 1874, p. 180). Here is the description, as accurate today as it was then:

The skin of the face and particularly of the eyelids became thick, semi-transparent and waxy. The face was generally pale, but had a delicate blush on the cheeks. The eyelids were swollen and ridged and hung down flaccidly on the cheeks. They did not pit on being squeezed. The skin was singularly dry. It was harsh and rough to the touch: the hairs were feebly developed, and no traces of fatty secretion could be found. Within two years, the complexion was pale yellow.

Today, over 80 per cent of people with primary failure of the thyroid gland ('primary hypothyroidism' in medical terms) have skin that is rough, dry and covered with fine scales. In around 10 per cent, the prominent change in appearance is wrinkles. You may think that the fairly sudden appearance of wrinkles is simply part of the ageing process. If they come with what you feel is a general slowing down of all your physical and mental activities, then you should consider a thyroid problem and ask your doctor about it.

Dr Gill, sadly, good doctor that he was, did not have the cure to hand for his patient. It was still some years before a thyroid extract was available to doctors. Today the diagnosis and its treatment are thankfully readily available.

For Belle, a simple blood test confirmed her thyroid failure. She was given a daily dose of thyroxine to take, and she soon felt much better. Her face changed back to its previous appearance, she started to brighten up, and she was soon out and about with her old friends. Her memory returned, and her mood lifted. It was an extremely simple way to cure memory loss, and she was very grateful for it.

Not all cases of a 'low thyroid' are as obvious as Belle's. My second example is of a doctor:

Elaine

For Elaine Brown, going back to work after having her first baby was the hardest thing she had ever done. She worried all the time about leaving him. Unsurprisingly, he cried every morning as Elaine dropped him off at the nursery: it took time for her to recover from the 'drenching panic' (her words) on her subsequent journey to work. A year later she found she was losing her hair. She blamed her hairdresser's new lotions for it, and even though she was a doctor, she didn't suspect for a moment that she might have a thyroid problem.

Life continued to be a struggle. Although she was working fewer hours than before, she felt that having a baby had 'dented her brain'. She became a regular visitor to her own doctor's surgery (we don't try to treat ourselves) for a series of minor complaints. Her inability to cope, her ebbing confidence, her gain in weight (she had put on nearly two stone) and her unruly and thinning hair were telling on her. At work she was forgetting routine things and finding it difficult to remember the names of drugs and times of appointments. She was very slow at making decisions.

She became pregnant again, and her second child was born two years after the first. Only now did it dawn on her that she needed medical help. Every task, from simply getting dressed to seeing a patient, had become a mountain to climb. She told her doctor that she was 'tired all the time' (we call this problem TATT for obvious reasons) and admitted the magnitude of her symptoms and the effect that they were having on her life at home and at work. A routine test for thyroid function showed that it was vanishingly small. She had all the problems of a low thyroid output without the obvious facial features of it – which was why she hadn't recognized it herself.

Elaine was delighted at the result, because she had thought she had depression – a much more difficult condition to treat. Once she was started on the replacement hormone, she brightened up within days, felt a million times better, and her confidence, her intellect, her memory and her previous excellent quality of life came flooding back. For the first time, she was able to enjoy her children and her job. She splits her week into a job share with another female doctor and has the great satisfaction of both bringing up her children and practising a high standard of medicine again.

Belle and Elaine are two ends of the wide spectrum of hypothyroidism, but they do have features in common, one of which is a deteriorating memory. So if you feel that your memory might have an underlying basis in thyroid failure, do mention it to your doctor. The blood test is simple and gives you a definite answer within a few days. Either you have it or you haven't, and if you have, you can be sure of a big boost when you start the treatment. Here is a list of symptoms (what you feel) and signs (what the doctor finds) in hypothyroidism. If you have several of them, see your doctor:

Symptoms	Signs
Feeling tired all the time	Slow movement
Lethargy/lassitude/laziness	Slow speech
Sleepiness at inappropriate times	Hoarse speech
Mental dullness and memory loss	Slow pulse
Depression	Dry skin
Intolerance to cold	Thickened, swollen skin of face and limbs
Weight gain	Lack of sweating
Loss of appetite	Less active reflexes
Constipation	Slower reflexes
Menstrual problems	Sometimes (not always) goitre (a swelling in the neck)
Joint pains	Abnormal sensations such as pins and needles and numbness

9

Depression and memory

A doctor reading Elaine's story (case history in the last chapter) would have had another diagnosis in mind before the thyroid problem was discovered – depression. Low thyroid activity mimics depression in many ways, which is why we test for it before we decide that depression is the real underlying cause of memory loss and mental slowness.

What is depression?

Anyone whose memory is deteriorating must be considered as a possible case of depression, which is why the staff at memory clinics, for example, ask new patients to complete a depression questionnaire to make sure that it isn't a strong underlying cause of their memory failure. This book isn't about depression, so I'll try to cover it in a single chapter – which is a tall order, because it's a massive subject to condense into a few words. But here goes:

It's normal to feel low from time to time. Everyone does. When circumstances are unpleasant, such as problems at work or arguments within a family, to feel unhappy is the usual, and even correct, reaction. It may be the stimulus to put things right, and that may be the reason we have moods at all. Without feeling low we would have no drive to get better. We take action to correct it, and the lower mood soon fades.

In the same way, it's normal to feel 'high' too. If things are going right, we are rewarded by feelings of pleasure, and even elation. We enjoy ourselves. During the normal routine of everyday life we are usually somewhere between the two, on an even keel, with a mood that is neither high nor low, but level.

Depression is a departure from the norm. The mood drops, out of the blue, with no apparent cause. You feel it, but find it difficult to pinpoint any preceding cause. Or you may think you know the cause, but when you try to explain it to friends or family, they are at a loss to understand.

And depression lasts. Most normal mood swings last a few hours, or a day or two at most. Depression continues long after that time. If you feel low for more than a week or so, and the mood stays with you all the time, hour after hour, you are depressed.

However, depression isn't just about mood. It affects almost every aspect of your life. You find that you wake up in the early hours of the morning, and can't get back to sleep again. You lose your enjoyment of the everyday things you cherish, like your garden or your favourite food or television programme. You don't have the energy to do things, such as take that daily walk. You are always too tired and weary. You lose your appetite, and some weight. It's rare to gain weight when you are depressed, but for a few, who are exercising much less than normally, it may happen.

You aren't as efficient at work or in doing things around the house. You blame yourself for all the things that are going wrong around you. You can't concentrate and take normal decisions about everyday things, such as what to buy when shopping or to make for dinner. Your memory for everyday tasks goes. You burn the food and become untidy. Even the way you walk and stand can change, so that you look 'low and slow' to other people. And your sex life disappears, as you lose all interest in your partner.

If that isn't enough, depression doesn't come alone as a symptom: you can become anxious, irritable, agitated and mentally slow, even to the point of seeming 'retarded' to your family and friends. If it persists, and becomes more severe, eventually you may stop eating, start thinking that people are against you (paranoia) and may even think of suicide.

You don't have to have all of the above symptoms to be diagnosed as depressed. But their pattern is plain: if you have had an episode of depression you will instantly recognize your particular bunch of symptoms, and you may well have experienced them all.

Yet it's rare for people to complain to their doctors that they are depressed. Often they 'somatize' their problems with a physical complaint. A common one is constipation – the bowel is slowed, too. Another is difficulty in sleeping. As we said earlier, most people with depression fall asleep as usual, but wake up in the early hours, and can't then get back to sleep. Failing to get to sleep in the first place is more a sign of anxiety than depression. If you have both anxiety and depression, then the result can be a mixture of both types of insomnia. I've known several patients whose complaint of memory difficulties (they were persuaded to come by their spouses) was the first and even only outward sign of depression.

Interestingly, psychiatrists and GPs differ in their experience of patients with anxiety and depression. Studies of in-patients in psychiatric hospitals strongly suggest that depression and anxiety are two distinct illnesses, and that the two don't overlap. This is certainly not the experience of GPs, many of whose patients show signs of both. GPs also feel that they can correlate the degree of depression with that of the anxiety, so that the deeper the depression, the worse is the patient's anxiety. Of course, there are people with only depression or only anxiety, but these diagnoses are not so easily distinguished by the patients, who tend not to differentiate between them. Ask yourself if you are more depressed than anxious, or the reverse, and you will see what I mean.

Suspecting depression

What makes the GP suspect acute depression when a patient is presenting with the condition for the first time? We have, broadly speaking, five main groups of patient in whom we put depression in the front line of diagnoses. Few of them use the word 'depression' when they are presenting their complaint. They are people:

- Who find they are not coping with their usual routine. They can't go to work, they can't even be bothered to get out of bed. Once they have struggled to dress, they can't look after the house.
- With vague symptoms that they can't describe well, such as tiredness, loss of appetite, loss of weight, problems with sleep.
- Who have turned to behaviour that isn't usual for them, such as drinking too much, taking drugs, or taking to rages and violent outbursts.
- Who have caused worry to their family or friends because their relationships have changed. Families may have become frustrated with them: there may be guilt feelings on both sides, and the family may have become less than sympathetic towards them.
- Who talk about committing suicide, and may have made detailed plans to do so.

On this last point, anyone who has mentioned suicide should be taken very seriously. The old wives' tale that people who threaten suicide never do it is wrong. People who talk about it are more likely to do it than people who don't. A threat of suicide is an emergency that needs immediate support from the psychiatric services.

The above list of typical ways in which depression presents is not exhaustive or exclusive. The patient who has repeated bouts of headache, backache, other muscle pains and dizzy spells may be diagnosed as having fibromyalgia or myalgic encephalopathy (well publicized as ME), but often has an underlying depression as a cause of the symptoms. Palpitations, breathlessness, nausea and excessive sweating are other signals of a hidden depression.

Many people, therefore, hide their true problem in a host of other symptoms. Why do they do this? One reason is that they may think that doctors are there to help them with physical problems, and are less experienced in mental ones. Another is that they really do have these physical symptoms. Physical and psychiatric problems like depression often do co-exist: it's just that the patient is more consciously concerned with the physical aspect of his or her illness. Yet a third reason is that, even in the twenty-first century, people believe that there is a social stigma in having a 'mental' disorder, and they are ashamed to admit they have one.

A good GP should be able to sift the physical from the mental symptoms and get to the heart of the illness. If it turns out to be depression, then there is a lot of explaining and reassuring to be done. The stigma must be removed, once and for all. If the patient continues to feel guilty, with low self-esteem, the chances of getting better are less.

Depression can occur at any age

Depression in the elderly

Depression occurs at any age, from childhood to old age, and age can make a difference to the form it takes. For example, it's common for people to assume that depression is a natural part of old age. As we slow down and become more infirm with age, so the argument goes, our brain slows too, and with it our mood. If that is natural, the reasoning continues, then there is nothing much we can do about it. But it isn't any more natural to become depressed in old age than it is in younger people. It's still an illness that we can try to reverse, regardless of age.

The main problem for depression in old age is that it's mistaken for dementia, a condition that is less easy to influence because it's the result of a true loss of brain capacity. It must be admitted that both illnesses start in a similar way. An older person who is difficult, stubborn, complains a lot, demands a lot of his or her family and carers, who is also forgetful, confused and living in the past, is often seen as having dementia, when in fact the cause is depression. And depression can respond just as well to treatment in the elderly as in younger adults.

There are clues to the difference between depression and dementia in the old. Dementia usually comes on gradually, the loss of reasoning power (cognition) is steady and present all the time, it steadily and noticeably progresses, and does not improve with treatment. Yet the patient with dementia is not unduly distressed by this deterioration, and retains a self-respect that is lost to the person with depression. Older people with depression have times when they are lucid and just as intelligent as they were, will respond to antidepressant measures (to be detailed in later chapters), are usually distressed by their state of mind and their memory problems, and have a very poor image of themselves.

Depression in children

Children can be depressed too. They are usually anxious as well, have difficulty sleeping, are irritable, refuse to eat, won't go to school, have phobias, complain of stomach pains, become obsessive about small things, are always complaining they feel ill (a true form of hypochondria) and may even think of suicide. Children showing some or all of these characteristics are in serious danger of self-harm. There is also a very high chance that they have been sexually abused.

Depression in teenagers

Teenagers are possibly the most vulnerable age group of all. We tend to *expect* teenagers to have emotional problems, so that too little may be made of their misery. It's common for them to be told to 'grow up', as if that could help in any way. Yet they are beset by self-doubt and agonize about whether or not they are accepted by their peers. They are often at odds with their parents, and are not yet mature enough to come to terms with their feelings. This age group is at high risk of suicide, and depressed teenagers present with the same set of physical and mental symptoms as adults. They should be cared for especially well if they are to come through this turbulent period in their lives unscathed.

Special cases of depression

Grief

Grief is a natural process that follows the death of a relative, partner or close friend. It has a surprisingly predictable pattern. For the first few days you are numb, and find it difficult to come to terms with the change in your life. The numbness lasts for a few days, usually until after the funeral. The 'pining' phase follows, in which you concentrate on your loss. You have a poor appetite, and you experience lapses in memory and concentration, and become irritable and depressed.

If the grief reaction intensifies after this period, you can feel despair and become disorganized in your home and at work. You even sense the dead person near you, a feeling that is most acute when you are near to sleep in the evenings. It may take up to a year for the most intense grief to start to settle: if that is your case, you will only begin to get over the worst after the first anniversary of the death, which is naturally always painful.

So grief has three phases. The first is a loss of normal emotional responses, and this can last a few days to a few weeks. The second is mourning proper, in which there is yearning for the dead person, somatic symptoms similar to those listed for other forms of depression, and even guilt and denial of death. In the third phase comes acceptance and readjustment to normal life. From phase one to phase three takes around six months for most people. If this process lasts longer, or is blocked by a too-stoic and repressed reaction to the bereavement, then the person needs urgent and continuing treatment. That means counselling, a process called cognitive behaviour therapy (CBT), often complemented by antidepressant drugs. Antidepressants are not given to help people through a normal grief reaction.

Postnatal depression

Giving birth is naturally an emotional time. Hopefully, most of the emotions are uplifting. Most pregnancies are happy affairs, and when they end in a healthy baby and mother (not to mention the father), they are an occasion for rejoicing, not depression.

So when a new mother becomes depressed it can be difficult for those around her to understand. Imagine how much worse it is for the mother herself, who has been looking forward to her baby and all the joys he or she is expected to bring, to find that she is in a deep black hole, from which she sees no escape. Add to that the great guilt she feels about being unhappy, her feeling that she does not love her baby as she should, and the total loss of self-esteem that accompanies that feeling, and you start to get the measure of postnatal depression.

It's almost normal to have postnatal 'blues' a few days after giving birth. Most experts now believe that they are the consequence of the steep fall in female sex hormones such as progesterone that occurs after the baby is born. Some women feel the 'blues' are similar to the premenstrual tension that occurs before their periods. If so, they may well share the same cause – progesterone levels fall just before each period starts. We know that there are progesterone receptors on the surface of brain cells, and it could well be that the fall in hormone levels directly alters the levels of the brain neurotransmitters mentioned in the last chapter. If so, this could explain the change in mood, and why it comes as an unexpected form of depression with no obvious cause. (The next chapter goes into changes in the brain cells in depression more thoroughly.)

Postnatal blues start when the baby is less than ten days old, and usually last only a day or two. The mother feels sad, often cries for no apparent reason, then recovers quite quickly. The blues are not a sign of impending postnatal depression: the two are not linked. True postnatal depression may start at any time up to three to four months after the birth. With it come all the depression symptoms described in the previous few pages. It's no different in type and range of severity from the depression suffered by other adults.

However, it does have one further and massive complication: the depressed mother has all the responsibilities that lie in having a new baby to look after. That can put a huge strain on the woman and her relationships with her partner and the rest of her immediate family and close friends. They all need to be extremely supportive, and careful not to apportion blame or guilt on to the mother.

Happily, postnatal depression usually responds well to treatment and is short lived. There is a one in seven chance of its returning after the next pregnancy, so that it's best for the woman to be well prepared the next time.

Many women report that they think their memories are particularly bad during pregnancy and the immediate period after the birth. They feel that their memories are worse than before their pregnancies, and that the loss covers all aspects of memory – including their everyday working memory and their memories of the recent and distant past. However, this feeling is temporary, and even false, because when they are given rigorous memory tests, they score normally. They just take longer to complete them. It seems that their hormone changes during pregnancy and for the few months afterwards slow their memories, but it does not wipe them out!

Seasonal affective disorder (SAD)

SAD receives a lot of publicity every winter, usually around the New Year. That's the time when newspaper editors are scratching around for a seasonal topic, having exhausted the stress of Christmas, the New Year resolutions and the annual 'flu epidemic. SAD makes a lot of column inches, too, in the women's magazines, often alongside advertisements for complementary and alternative medicines as winter 'pick-me-ups'.

The odd thing about SAD is that although there is so much publicity about it, surgery attendances for depression don't seem to vary much throughout the year. In fact, they drop away around Christmas and New Year, as families get together and the seasonal spirit cheers people up. So, many family doctors are less convinced than the rest of the public that SAD makes a big contribution to the numbers of people with depression. The World Health Organization has yet to define it. However, the Americans have issued their guidelines on how to make the diagnosis of SAD. For what it's worth, here it is:

SAD should be diagnosed if the patient has had at least three periods of depression in three different winter seasons of which at least two should be consecutive. These depressive illnesses should occur within the same 60-day winter period in each year. The patient's winter depressions should be three or more times more common than his or her depressions occurring at other times in the year.

It's difficult to substantiate this pattern of depression in any patient. In my rural practice in the West of Scotland, in which daylight lasted only seven hours in mid-winter and it was hardly dark at all in high summer, the peak monthly number of prescriptions for depression was almost always in May. In May there are an average of 15 daylight hours in the 24. Over the five years in which I was the only doctor in the practice, the peak antidepressant prescription rate was never in the months of December to February.

Of course, this is anecdotal evidence from one practice, and is not enough on which to base judgement on whether SAD is a separate form of depression from the other types. However, it's a pointer that at least in our area it is not a significant illness. I would still agree that if people have truly seasonal depression, which hits in the wintertime and eases off in the summer, they should be offered light therapy along with all the standard treatments for depression.

Alcohol

In describing the various forms of depression, I cannot leave out alcohol. A classic way in which patients with hidden depression present themselves to their doctors is with alcohol abuse. If you are depressed, it's tempting to turn to alcohol to 'drown your sorrows'. The phrase is much used, and with good reason, in normal conversation. But there is another side to alcohol and depression. Even if you started drinking just because you like the 'buzz' it gives you, and not because you were depressed, it will leave you with a lowered mood.

Alcohol is not a 'pick-me-up' – far from it. It's much more a 'let-me-down'. Alcohol abuse not only worsens an already depressive illness, it can even initiate it. For a short while, alcohol may lighten your mood and loosen your inhibitions, but within as short a time as an hour, that passes. Then you can have many hours of misery as the hangover sets in. If you drink regularly, you are always slightly hung over. This is not just a social thing: alcohol is a powerful drug that slows the brain and directly lowers the mood. All alcoholics are unhappy, no matter how cheerful they seem to be on the surface. If you have a tendency towards depression, the wise answer is to control your drinking. A glass of wine with a meal is fine. Several glasses of any alcoholic drink each day is not.

Alcohol really hits your memory with devastating blows. 'Korsakoff syndrome' is a particular form of memory loss that is caused by alcohol abuse. It involves loss of recent memory, so that sufferers are constantly repeating phrases and sentences over and over again. Obviously, the condition is recognized very easily by the people close to them, and it's one of the ways in which alcohol abusers eventually find their way to their doctors. By the time they have the full-blown Korsakoff syndrome, alcohol has damaged substantial areas of the brain and the liver. The only answer is to stop drinking completely and hope that these two most vital organs will show some degree of recovery. In my experience, that's rare.

10

Treating memory loss linked to depression

If your memory problems have been diagnosed as being due to depression, then you will need treatment for the depression itself, along with the good memory management described in the previous pages. The modern treatment for depression involves two complementary approaches – drugs to restore the normal balance in the brain of the 'neurotransmitter' chemicals that are thought to cause it, and cognitive behaviour therapy (CBT), in which you will be asked to change your way of thinking about things.

Antidepressant drugs

Around half of all people being treated with drugs for their depression are still being treated with the original 'tricyclic' antidepressant drugs. They are called this because of the three-ringed chemical structure. Each drug differs from all the others in its dose, how often it should be given, and how quickly you feel an improvement once you start taking it. They also differ in their side-effect rates and severity. However, neither you nor your GP can predict how a particular tricyclic will affect you. What suits one person may not suit another. Often it's a case of trial and error until you and your GP find the one that helps to lift your mood with the fewest and mildest side-effects.

Most of the other half of the population taking medication for depression are on one of the many 'selective serotonin reuptake inhibitors' (SSRIs). There's no need to go into detailed explanation here of what SSRIs mean: it's enough to state that they increase the levels in the brain of serotonin, one of the neurotransmitters thought to be at lower than normal concentrations in the brain in depression. A small minority of people are taking different drugs that act on other neurotransmitters (for the technically minded, these neurotransmitters are called noradrenaline, acetylcholine and dopamine).

As with the tricyclics, it may take time to find the drug that suits you. Your GP and your practice nurse will help you through the first few months until you find the best treatment.

Whatever the drug that is chosen for you, it's vital that you understand one thing. You will begin to feel better, hopefully after a week or two (don't expect instant relief). When you do, *don't* think of stopping the drug. Your depression is not cured, it's just being managed. If you stop your course of drugs early, you may well experience a 'rebound' in your symptoms, so that you descend steeply back into a deep depression. Most doctors, once they have started to prescribe an antidepressant for a patient, will insist on at least six months of treatment.

My own experience suggests that a two-year course is preferable, and probably the minimum for most patients. It can take that time to help your brain adjust and for your depression not to return when the drugs are stopped. So don't expect to come off your drugs early.

Never stop the drugs yourself. Always seek your GP's advice before changing the dose or stopping. People who stop the drugs abruptly can experience serious withdrawal symptoms, such as nightmares and severe swings in mood. You need help and supervision when you eventually stop the course.

Cognitive behaviour therapy (CBT)

We all have to face life-shaking problems from time to time. Something hits us out of the blue, like a physical illness in ourselves or a member of our family, or the death of someone close. Or there is a sudden unexpected shift in our financial state, like losing a well-paid job, or our expected pension disappears because of a stock market crash (a very common life event in the early twenty-first century). Or there is a marital disagreement, separation or divorce. Or a family row isolates us: inter-sibling arguments sometimes seem like wars.

How we face up to all these unwanted events depends on the other four aspects of our characters:

1 What we think. Are our thoughts helpful or unhelpful at such times?
2 Our emotional response. Do we show the most appropriate emotions (logic, reason, cool-headedness) when unwanted events arise, or do we react with inappropriate ones such as anger, resentment, suspicion or panic?
3 Our physical response. Do we get physical symptoms such as palpitations, breathlessness, indigestion, nausea or diarrhoea?
4 How we behave. Do we become introverted and withdrawn, or do we become overactive and antisocial? Maybe we start throwing things.

Do you recognize yourself already? If you do, that's a start. Take a little time to think about the way you respond to such 'life events'. Try to stand outside yourself and assess your responses in an unbiased way. Ask yourself three questions:

1 How well do I manage unpleasant thoughts or feelings?
2 How assertive am I when faced with unwanted events and pressures?
3 How good am I in finding practical solutions to my problems?

Now see how you match up with a few common problems.

Examples of how cognitive behaviour therapy can work

Thinking you are being snubbed by someone

Let's take an example. You are in the supermarket and you see someone you know in the same aisle. He or she passes you without stopping to say hello. What is your first reaction? Is it to think that she saw you but has pretended not to, because she doesn't like you? Because of that, do you feel terrible? Does that then make you cut short your shopping and go home, to be miserable by yourself? And does that make you feel drained, tired, listless and even nauseated and sick? Do you find you have palpitations, and then can't get to sleep that night?

This sequence of events may seem laughable to people who have never been depressed. They would simply assume that the other person didn't see them, or was too busy, or perhaps too preoccupied with his or her own emotional difficulties to stop to chat. Even if they thought that the other person was really trying to avoid them, they would put the blame for that on the other person and forget it. How would a 'normal' person react to the imagined snub? By going forward and saying hello regardless, thus breaking any barrier, imagined or real.

However, the sequence is no laughing matter to people who are, or who have been, depressed. They see this behaviour as typical of their own when they are depressed. They remember acting in exactly this way, many times. Analyse what has happened.

First, there was the problem that you had to face – being ignored, or not noticed in the supermarket by a friend. Look on this as a minor life event that stimulates your subsequent thoughts, your mental and physical reactions, and behaviour.

Second, there was your immediate reasoning following the encounter. You assumed a deliberate snub, and blamed yourself for it. That's as negative as you can get! You reacted with suspicion (that you were not liked), with a downturn in mood (misery), and perhaps anger.

Third, your mental reaction created physical distress: tiredness, weakness, 'sick in your stomach', lost appetite, a fast heart rate (palpitations) and sleeplessness.

Fourth, you took inappropriate actions: you cut short your shopping, went home, and kept away from other people. You did not want to share your feelings with anyone else.

All this was because someone you knew failed to acknowledge you in the supermarket. If you could step outside yourself and without bias look at this series of events, you would see how wrong your attitudes and actions are, and how much you need to correct them.

That is what cognitive behaviour therapy is all about. It's to help you understand how you think when you are depressed (that's the cognitive part), and then to know how to change that thinking and your subsequent behaviour accordingly (that's the behaviour part). The good thing about this is that when you do alter your behaviour, your mood lifts. One often follows the other, like day follows night. In fact, that's frequently how people who manage to change their everyday behaviour often describe the change in their depression. One patient described it as 'coming out of the dark into the sunshine'. First comes the behaviour change, then comes the lift in mood.

We can take that supermarket encounter again as an example. Suppose instead of thinking the worst, you had gone up to your friend and broken the ice. She might have reacted by apologizing: that morning she had broken her glasses, and most faces were fuzzy to her. She just hadn't recognized you. So you have coffee together, promise to meet up on another shopping day, and maybe have lunch. Instead of going home alone, worrying and getting in a physical 'state', you get home in a good mood, looking forward to your next meeting and planning ahead what you might do together. That night you sleep well. No nausea, no weakness, no tiredness, no loss of appetite, no fast heartbeats, no misery. All because you reacted healthily to the 'event'.

So how do you start to change things? The first priority is to examine the types of event that might trigger your depressive reaction. Recognize first of all that no life is without its problems. What you must learn to do is to understand where those problems are for you, and how you can best deal with them.

Money worries

Problems mainly come under three headings – money, marital and friends, and job worries. We all have them to some extent: an unfortunate few have problems in all these areas, and they can become overwhelming.

Take money first. A recent survey in Britain reported that, on average, people who are in debt owe a sum equivalent to 14 times their monthly income. That rises to 40 times in people on lower incomes in poorer districts. It's not surprising that people with these sorts of financial worries become depressed. If there is no way to increase your income, it's very difficult to see how you can get out of such debt. Nor is it difficult to understand why they become very depressed, and why they tend to forget things – they don't want to remember the circumstances in which they find themselves.

So how can you try to resolve your state of mind? The debt is the 'life event' (like the snub in the supermarket). You react to it negatively, by blaming yourself and feeling miserable. Or you respond with anger, blaming someone else for your predicament (like a partner in a low-paid job). Then you can't sleep, get headaches, feel vaguely sick, argue with people, especially those who are closest to you. And you don't even begin to pay off the debt, so that it mounts, week by week.

Recognize the scenario? It can only be resolved by facing up to it and this means seeking help. There are Citizens' Advice

Bureaux (CAB) in every district in Britain. Their counsellors will help you to organize your life by sorting out your repayments and advising on how best to economize on your expenses and outgoings. You will be amazed how just one visit to a CAB counsellor can lift your spirits. Anyone who wants to know how a CAB counsellor can help might remember the programmes put out by BBC TV's Alvin Hall as money adviser. He showed in the summer of 2003 just how seriously in debt people can get, and how it destroys their relationships, their self-belief and their peace of mind. Alvin is a great cognitive behaviour therapist, although he may not apply that label to himself.

'Marital' matters

We now turn to 'marital' matters. You will probably not admit it to your GP or your nurse adviser, and certainly not to your CAB counsellor, if you are having problems with sex. Yet most marriages that founder, founder on that rock. It's assumed that men want sex more often than women, and that for them it's just a physical thing, for self-gratification. Women, so the popular idea goes, need to be wooed, to have some romance, before they can be ready for sex. And they can't become enthusiastic about it if they are tired and anxious after a day of depression and stress.

Yet that isn't necessarily true. Disagreements about sex may come from your loss of sex drive, a common symptom of depression and lack of self-esteem. And that is transmitted to your partner. Problems with sexual relationships between partners are fairly evenly split between the male and female. Depressed men are just as likely to lose their sex drive as their female partners, and this can be a source of frustration for both of them. It can also be a source of anger and resentment, and deteriorating relationships, that can't be solved without professional help.

Does the depression come before the loss of sex drive, or vice versa? It's the old question of the chicken or the egg. Whichever way round it is, the answer is to face the problem, just as with all the others, and try to solve it reasonably. Talking about it to your partner is essential, but if that isn't helping, and there are resentments on both sides (there often are), then you need to agree to go together to someone who can help. Sometimes that is your doctor, or a specialist member of the family doctor team. If that isn't comfortable for you both, then an outside counsellor who doesn't know you can help. There is no need for such counsellors to be knowledgeable about the treatment of depression: they are specifically there to help with the sexual problem.

By now you will be realizing that cognitive behaviour therapy is a very practical way of looking at your depression. It examines your circumstances and your flawed response to them, and tries to correct it. In doing so, it should lift your mood and help you understand yourself more clearly.

So forget your depression and your memory problems for a moment, and think of yourself and how you react to circumstances. Read the following statements, and see how many 'yes' answers you give to them:

- I have frequent arguments with my partner or closest relative.
- I can't really talk to this person about my problems.
- There isn't anyone I can talk to.
- I'm always under stress managing my home/partner/children/dependent parents.
- I have debts that I can't see myself ever clearing.
- I'm away from my roots, and don't like the district I live in.
- I don't get on with my neighbours.
- I'm having difficulties at work – with colleagues and with keeping up with work demands.

- I don't like my job – or I can't get a job and I am worried about it.

Two or more 'yes' answers and you need help

These are all negative thoughts, suggesting that you are seeing everything from a negative viewpoint. That needs to change – and cognitive behaviour therapy should help you to change it. If you recognize yourself in the last two chapters, please see your doctor, not for your memory loss, but to treat your depression.

11

Your circulation – small strokes and memory loss

It goes without saying that for the brain to function at its optimum it needs good blood flow through it – it needs smooth artery walls, no obstructions, and blood passing within them at the correct pressure and fluidity. As we age, artery walls can roughen and narrow, the pressure can rise, and the blood thicken – all of which can eventually end in a lack of oxygen supply to vital areas of the brain.

Strokes and memory loss

Blood clots can form on the roughened areas of artery, or higher than normal pressure within it can rupture its walls, so that blood leaks through into the brain substance beyond it.

Both of these processes cause what we all know as strokes, the first being a 'thrombotic', or clotting, stroke, the second being a 'haemorrhagic', or bleeding, stroke. Both can be devastating and life-threatening: most of us fear strokes, because we see how they can leave people with permanent disabilities.

What fewer of us know is that we can have tiny, minor, strokes that happen fairly frequently, without us knowing that we have had them or making us feel particularly ill. They are caused by small clots of blood travelling through the brain's circulation, only to get 'stuck' in the smallest arteries at the surface of the brain – the cortex you read about in earlier chapters. Each time a clot does this, it destroys the tiny area of brain that would have been supplied by the now blocked artery. And each time, a little memory is lost. Multiply this by hundreds of times and you can understand how, eventually, you can gradually lose your memory, bit by bit, over several years. You may not notice this yourself, but eventually your family and work colleagues will begin to realize that you are 'losing something' and will advise you to see your doctor. He or she is sure to examine you fully and, in doing so, will become aware that the problem lies in your circulation.

The condition is called 'multi-infarct memory loss' ('infarct' means the death of tissue beyond a clot in an artery) and it's explained in the next few pages. Although the memory loss is directly caused by damage to the arteries in the brain, the source of the clots that cause the blockages is usually in the heart or the main arteries in the neck leading from the heart to the brain – the carotid arteries.

To explain how this happens, I need first of all to describe what happens to our circulation as we grow older. We begin with smooth arteries, a heart that pumps normally at the right pressure, and a good circulation through the heart, the brain and the rest of our body. But it doesn't stay like that for long. The way we live – what we eat, whether we smoke or not, whether our blood pressure rises or not, the kind of fats in our blood that we inherit from our parents, how much exercise we do – all conspire together to thicken our artery walls, damage their smooth linings, make the blood flowing through them stickier (more viscous), and more liable to clot. If we become obese, the fats in our blood tend to stick to the walls and be deposited in them, making us liable to experiencing clots and haemorrhages. If along with the obesity we become diabetic, the higher circulating levels of sugar and other abnormalities (for example, high levels of insulin) can double and even treble the risk of artery damage and blood clotting. If we smoke, the risks of blood clotting inside the arteries multiplies more than tenfold. If you add all these together, then we are sitting on a time-bomb. It is small wonder that one in three deaths in developed countries are caused by strokes and heart attacks. Sometimes they happen out of the blue, sometimes we have warnings beforehand – and multi-infarct memory loss is one of those warnings.

The disease process in our arteries – atheroma

By far the most common cause of narrowed arteries in the heart, in the main arteries such as the carotids, and in the brain is 'atheroma'. Taken from the ancient Greek word for 'porridge', it describes a process of fatty deposits in the artery walls. In the early stages, all that can be seen are fatty streaks in the inner surface of the arteries. American army doctors in Korea were astonished to find that they already existed in the arteries of young soldiers killed in action – by the age of 18, most of the men had them. In the later stages of atheroma, these 'plaques' – roughened, lumpy, thickened, inflamed patches – project into the centre of the arteries. They are not unlike the deposits of chalk inside a water pipe in a hard-water area.

Not only do plaques narrow the arteries, slowing the flow of blood through them, they also cause eddy currents beyond them – and they can damage the artery wall further. The disturbance in smooth flow also makes the blood more prone to clotting. A clot, or thrombosis, can develop to block the whole artery. If that is in a coronary artery in the heart, it causes a heart attack due to 'coronary thrombosis': if it's in a brain artery, it causes a stroke. Clots forming on plaques in the carotid arteries in the neck can break off and be swept into the brain – and that is the main cause of multi-infarct memory loss.

The three main causes of atheroma are smoking, uncontrolled high blood pressure, and high fat levels in the blood ('hyper-lipidaemia'). If you are overweight, take very little exercise, and/or have diabetes, you are at higher than normal risk of having atheroma, mainly because all three are linked with high blood pressure and hyperlipidaemia.

Smoking

If you smoke, it's vital that you understand why smoking is such a lethal habit for you. The three main ingredients of smoke are tars, nicotine and carbon monoxide. All three promote angina. The tars (which contain thousands of harmful chemicals), by damaging the delicate lung cells, prevent maximum uptake of oxygen into the blood from the lungs. They can also, of course, initiate lung cancer. The chemicals in the tars are thought to act directly on artery walls, producing the inflammation that causes plaques of atheroma to form and worsen.

Nicotine is one of the most powerful of all poisons. It narrows small arteries by causing the muscles in their walls to go into spasm. That applies to all arteries, including those in the eyes, brain, kidneys, limbs and coronary arteries. The effect can be measured even in a once-a-day smoker. Anything that has the potential to narrow an already narrowed coronary, carotid or cerebral artery (in the brain) even further is obviously a danger.

Carbon monoxide is a poison to the red blood cells and heart muscles, and to many other vital processes in cells, including the lining cells of arteries. Its main disadvantage for the smoker is that red blood cells and heart muscle cells take carbon monoxide, rather than oxygen, up from the lungs. If you smoke 20 cigarettes a day, around a fifth of your red blood cells and heart muscle cells are not working efficiently. That can be crucial if your heart needs extra oxygen when you increase your exercise level.

Cigarette smoking also increases the amount of fibrinogen in the blood. Fibrinogen is the body's natural defence against injury to blood vessels – it instigates clotting. So an increase in fibrinogen substantially raises your risk of a clot forming inside a coronary or cerebral artery. It's thought that many sudden deaths in smokers are due exactly to that. It's also clear that smoking is very closely linked to multi-infarct memory loss, which eventually becomes multi-infarct dementia as it progresses.

Stopping smoking will hugely reduce the number of clots entering your brain arteries and will slow down the progress of further memory loss.

So if you have multi-infarct memory loss you *must* become a non-smoker from now on. Having read this, you have had your last cigarette. It's no use saying you will try to stop or that you will cut down. Even one cigarette a day is too many. Realize that you have to choose between cigarettes and life, and the decision is easy.

High blood pressure (hypertension)

The higher your blood pressure, the greater the damage it can cause to your blood vessels. It's linked with faster development of atheroma and thickening of the blood vessel walls, which naturally narrows their internal diameter – leaving much less space through which the blood can flow. This happens just as much to coronary and cerebral arteries as to any other artery. The more narrow the arteries, the greater the force the heart has to exert in order to keep the blood flowing through them – which means the blood pressure rises again, in a vicious circle.

So if you have high blood pressure with multi-infarct memory loss, it's essential to lower it and to keep it in the normal range. For every 1 per cent fall you can manage in your blood pressure, your risk of a heart attack or stroke falls by 2 per cent.

Your blood pressure can be lowered by changing your lifestyle (more exercise, eating healthily, coping better with stress, stopping smoking) and by taking antihypertensive (blood pressure-lowering) drugs. Your doctor will advise you on all these steps, and you will be asked to have your pressure checked once a month. Do not miss your blood pressure checks, because you cannot tell from how you feel how high it is. Many people with high blood pressure feel perfectly normal, and assume that they are fine. Tragically, their first symptom may be a heart attack or stroke – and by then it may be too late.

Hyperlipidaemia

The diagnosis of hyperlipidaemia is made from a blood test. This measures various types of fat, or lipid, in the blood, in units of millimoles per litre (mmol/l). The test result most often quoted is 'total cholesterol', which encompasses all the forms of fats. This may be subdivided into 'low density lipoprotein cholesterol', or LDL; 'high density lipoprotein cholesterol', or HDL; 'very low density lipoprotein', VLDL; and 'triglycerides'. Recently, further subdivisions have included 'apo-E lipoprotein' (apo-E).

It's enough here to know that high levels of LDL, VLDL and triglycerides are linked with severe atheroma, and that high levels of HDL protect against atheroma. The aim of treatment in people with hyperlipidaemia is to try to correct these figures – to lower LDL, VLDL and triglycerides, and to raise HDL levels.

There are several ways to do this. One is to eat foods containing fats and oils that promote formation of HDL and reduce LDL and VLDL levels. They include vegetable oils and oily fish. They should be eaten in preference to foods containing animal fats, such as red meats and full-fat dairy products. Another way is to exercise as much as you can. A third method is to take blood lipid-lowering tablets every day.

For many people with hyperlipidaemia (usually defined by doctors as a total cholesterol of 5.2 mmol/l or more), eating more healthily makes only a small difference to their basic blood lipid levels. They must add a blood-lipid-lowering drug. The West of Scotland Coronary Prevention Study (WOSCOPS), which followed up thousands of middle-aged men in the West of Scotland, showed that lowering total cholesterol levels with 'statin' drugs reduced their chances of heart attack and stroke between 25 per cent and 40 per cent.

Diabetes

People with either type of diabetes (early onset, needing insulin; or later onset, managed with diet and perhaps pills) are prone to accelerated atheroma. This is probably due to a mixture of problems, including big swings in blood glucose and high blood pressure. Consequently, if you have diabetes, you should be particularly careful to keep both your glucose and blood pressure under strict control. The nearer to normal your pressure and glucose are, the less likely you are to have severe atheroma, and therefore a heart attack or stroke.

This is particularly true for females. Women with diabetes have the same risk of angina and heart disease as men of the same age: they have lost their natural advantage over men. Non-diabetic women seem to be protected against atheroma, to the extent that the arteries of women in their sixties have a similar burden of atheroma to arteries of men in their fifties. In effect, atheroma is ten years slower in development in women than in men. This protection seems to be produced by the monthly rise and fall in the female hormones oestrogen and progesterone. Once the protection of these hormones is lost with the menopause, women's hearts and blood vessels are at exactly the same risk as men's. Poorly controlled diabetes and high blood pressure removes the protection that their hormones give them.

Assessing your risk factors

Given all that has been written above, it still happens that people with none of the risk factors (non-smoking men and women with normal blood pressure, with a total cholesterol below 5 mmol/l, who exercise regularly and do not have diabetes) develop multi-infarct memory loss. This is unfortunate, but it's very rare. Only 1 per cent of people with atheroma severe enough to cause circulation problems do not possess one of the risk factors, but if that 1 per cent is you, you should still be managed properly. How that is done is described in the following pages.

Diagnosing memory loss associated with multiple infarcts

If you have memory loss that is possibly associated with multiple infarcts, you will be given a full examination and a barrage of tests. You will be asked about common symptoms of atheroma, the commonest of all being pains in the chest, or angina. Such pain is brought about by atheroma in the coronary arteries, which are the arteries that feed the heart with oxygen. If you have angina, you will be asked:

1 When does your pain start?
2 What brings it on?
3 Does it ever come on when you are at rest?
4 Does it wake you at night?
5 What settles it?
6 Where exactly is the pain ?
7 What exactly does it feel like?
8 What other symptoms have you?
9 Do you get breathless or excessively tired?
10 Do you feel generally well?

This isn't a book on heart disease, so I won't go into more detail about it here, but the answers to these questions will guide your doctor towards or away from a diagnosis of angina. If your main problem is memory loss, the physical examination (listening to the chest, taking the pulse and blood pressure) may not reveal any problem (except, perhaps, a heart valve problem, or an enlarged heart). The straight X-ray is rarely helpful either.

If there is any reason for there to be doubt about your coronary arteries you will be asked to have an electrocardiograph (ECG). At rest, that too may show nothing abnormal, but an exercise ECG (done while you are walking on a treadmill) may tell a different story. Certain ECG changes start to show some time before you start to have pain or discomfort in the chest – and that indicates angina. You may also be asked to wear an ECG for 24 or 48 hours, while you go about your daily routine. This 'Holter monitoring' can help to decide how many periods of angina your heart experiences during the day and night, and how often, if at all, its rhythm is abnormal. Sometimes the Holter monitor shows periods of poor oxygen supply to the heart when you feel nothing wrong. This 'silent angina' has to be taken into account when decisions on how to treat the heart are made. Silent angina is particularly common in people with diabetes.

Armed with all this information, the doctor's task is to find out if there is a site in the coronary arteries where a blockage can be relieved. For that, you may be asked to have an angiogram. This technique involves injecting a dye into the coronary arteries via a catheter inserted into an arm or leg. It shows how wide the coronary arteries are, and where any narrowing (stenosis) may be. That allows the cardiologist to decide whether or not to intervene.

You may also be asked to undergo cardiac ultrasound tests ('echocardiography'): these do not involve needles or tubes. They show how the heart moves with each beat, giving a picture of the efficiency of the heart valves and the muscle.

You may also need a gamma camera scan: this involves injection of a tiny amount of radioactive material (not enough to harm you). It tells whether or not there is any area of the heart that is not contracting properly, as a result of a previous heart attack or longstanding angina. Nowadays cardiac surgeons can do much for hearts with areas that are contracting poorly – from surgery to remove the weak area, to fashioning 'wrap-around' supports from the chest wall muscles.

Why should all this be needed for someone whose problem (memory loss) is obviously in the brain, rather than the heart? Remember the source of the clots that arrive in the brain? They may have come from a heart that has not been beating properly. That can show up as an abnormal rhythm on the Holter monitor, or as a distortion in the way the heart beats on the echocardiography or scan. If a heart is not beating correctly, the blood may not flow through it smoothly and a clot may form within one of the chambers. Bits of the clot can break off and be swept up through the carotids into the brain – causing the process that leads to the memory loss.

Managing multi-infarct memory loss

Don't be surprised, therefore, if you are asked to take drugs to prevent the clots forming. One is common aspirin – one 75 mg tablet is enough per day to help prevent clots. It does so by making the 'platelets' – fragments of white blood cells that stick together to initiate clots in arteries – less 'sticky'. With aspirin, they tend not to clump together or to stick to the sides of the artery walls – and they lower the risk of clotting accordingly.

Another drug is warfarin. This blocks one of the essential steps in the process of blood clotting. Warfarin is more difficult to manage because the dose needs to be kept closely within certain limits – not so much that it causes excessive bleeding, and not so little that it makes no difference. Most people on warfarin have to have blood tests once, twice or four times a month to make sure they are on the correct dose.

Since we started to give our patients with circulation problems aspirin and warfarin, we have brought down their stroke levels by more than half – a huge achievement. How much that improvement has also been due to patients improving their lifestyles is still a matter of debate. I suspect the lifestyle changes are crucial.

The aim of treatment for multi-infarct memory loss is not just to improve the memory: it is also to avoid, or at least postpone for many years, a heart attack or stroke. This can only be done by co-operation between you and your family doctor's health care team. It involves *you* taking control of your lifestyle: the team will help with your medical management.

Looking for a new lifestyle

Once the diagnosis of multi-infarct disease has been made, the rules are simple:

- Don't smoke, not even one cigarette, not ever. And avoid smoky places. Even passive smoking is harmful to you, and could provoke a stroke.
- Don't be a couch potato. You can exercise up to your limits several times a week. Take advice about how much you can do from your doctor.
- Avoid circumstances that might bring on a break-up of a clot. Exercise is generally good, but for some people a *sudden* increase in excessive exercise can promote the break-up of a clot. Straining to pass a constipated stool is the famous example – it is how George IV died. 'Excessive' exercise in your case may be running, heavy gardening, lifting, climbing stairs, running for a bus, even exposure to the cold. Keep your house warm in winter and wear warm clothes outdoors.
- Don't eat too much at any one time. Small meals frequently, rather than big meals at long intervals apart, should be your rule.
- Don't drink too much alcohol. There's no harm in one or two drinks in 24 hours – but stick to that. More alcohol than that raises blood pressure and harms the heart muscle.
- React well to stress: don't get angry or anxious, as these two

emotions may provoke a sudden increase in blood pressure. If you are in a stressful job, think about changing it.

- Don't sacrifice yourself to your work – take proper time off, and enjoy your leisure.
- Keep your weight within normal limits – at least within a stone of the expected weight for your height. Being overweight raises the workload on your heart.
- Don't carry heavy weights or do anything that makes you strain while holding your breath. That's called the 'Valsalva' manoeuvre, and it can put an extra strain on your heart and push a clot from the heart into the brain (or into your lungs). For the same reason, avoid constipation.

Medical help

Medication

The drugs prescribed to help your heart have several aims. The purpose of nitrates is to open up your coronary arteries. They are designed to be dissolved under the tongue, or as patches to be stuck on the skin, or as tablets to be swallowed. Make sure that you follow the instructions very carefully, as too high a dose can provoke headaches (because they open up the arteries in the brain too) and sudden fainting when standing up from a sitting position (because they can cause the blood pressure to drop steeply).

Aspirin

Aspirin, taken as a single dose of 75 mg (a quarter of a standard aspirin), each day prevents the first step in thrombosis, so that it can stop a coronary or cerebral thrombosis. If you start to have persistent severe pain, and think you are having a heart attack, then take a whole 300 mg aspirin. This should minimize the volume of heart muscle affected. There is some evidence it will do the same if taken early in the course of a thrombotic stroke.

Once you have had a heart attack or a thrombotic stroke, aspirin 75 mg a day is likely to be given for the rest of your life. It may or may not be prescribed if you have had a haemorrhagic stroke. Much depends on your doctor's assessment on future risk and whether the risk of a further bleed is greater than future clots.

Blood pressure-lowering drugs like diuretics, betablockers, calcium antagonists, ACE inhibitors, and alpha-1 blockers, among others, all aim to reduce the force of the heartbeat, and therefore lower the workload of the heart. There are subtle differences between them in their effects and side-effects, which your doctor will discuss with you. For example, diuretics make you pass more urine than usual, so they are usually given in the morning, rather than in the evening, for obvious reasons.

Betablockers

These may provoke a wheeze, so they are not usually given to people with asthma. They can also narrow the blood vessels in the limbs, resulting in pale and cold fingers and toes – some people stop betablockers because of this side-effect.

Calcium antagonists

These work better if they are given in long-acting form, so that one tablet a day each morning lasts for 24 hours. Some calcium antagonists make you flush for the first few days of taking them: this unwanted effect can make some people stop taking them.

ACE inhibitors

ACE inhibitors often cause a dry cough, but if this can be tolerated they are very effective in angina with high blood pressure. Newer drugs that work in a similar way, but do not cause a cough, are angiotensin-II blockers. They may be preferred instead. If you have diabetes, then an ACE inhibitor is probably your drug of choice.

Alpha-1 blockers

These are a new approach to high blood pressure: they need to be given with caution to begin with, as they can sometimes cause too steep a fall in pressure to begin with, and make you faint. They are usually started on a low dose, which is gradually increased.

Anti-arrhythmic drugs

You may also be given these to prevent or reverse heartbeats that are irregular, too fast or too slow. Many people with angina are given a combination of drugs, to tackle the problems from different directions. One arrhythmia in particular, atrial fibrillation, is linked with multi-infarct memory loss. If you have this you will almost certainly be asked to take warfarin for the rest of your life.

Surgery

I mentioned earlier that the clots entering the brain to cause multi-infarct memory loss often arise from the carotid arteries. If your doctor suspects that they are the source of your problem, you will be asked to have a carotid angiogram. This X-ray procedure highlights the smoothness (or otherwise) of the lining of the arteries in the neck. If they are shown to be narrowed and to have clots on their surfaces, you will be offered an operation to remove the offending material: this is a 'carotid endarterectomy'.

The results are excellent, and reduce to virtually zero the numbers of infarcts you would have been exposed to without the surgery. Afterwards you will need to have warfarin treatment to prevent the clots re-forming.

A few words on angina

Although it's a medical word, angina has entered normal English as a well-known description of the pain in the chest linked with heart disease. Most people recognize that it may be the precursor to a full-blown heart attack. Less well known is the fact that chronic pain and discomfort due to coronary disease often leads to lethargy, a very poor quality of life, anxiety and depression, and along with all these comes memory disturbance. Today, many people find that surgery to improve the heart's function and the coronary circulation gives them a big 'lift', and not just physically. With the physical well-being comes a mental boost too, making that person feel much more at ease with life and helping with mood and memory. Time after time I've heard it said by patients who have had heart surgery that it was only after their operations that they realized how ill they had been feeling, now that they were feeling 'normal' again.

I have therefore included a final few paragraphs on the surgical treatment of angina, so that, if you are facing it, you will feel less anxious about it.

Surgical procedures to treat angina

Everyone has now heard of bypass grafts and balloon angioplasty. In the first, the surgeon takes a piece of vein from a leg, or an artery from inside the chest wall, and creates a 'bypass' for blood to flow through them around the narrowed segment of coronary artery. The operation has been amazingly successful over the years, with many people enjoying a much improved quality of life, with much less pain or even no pain at all. Age is no barrier: many people over the age of 70 have had bypass grafts with great success.

Bypass grafts entail a hospital stay of around ten days and a further eight weeks of gradually increasing exercise and a return to normal activities.

Balloon angioplasty entails the cardiologist inserting a catheter (a fine flexible tube) into an artery in the elbow, from where it's passed up into the aorta, and then into the affected coronary artery, under X-ray control. Just behind the tip of the catheter is a deflated balloon. The tip is passed through the narrowed segment of artery, so that the balloon is precisely at the stenosis. Then it is blown up. This flattens out the offending atheromatous plaque, so that the arterial lining is smooth again. Blood flows through without disturbance and without the eddies that might provoke a thrombosis or a tear. Angioplasty is done under sedation, but not an anaesthetic, and entails a much shorter stay in hospital than bypass grafts. It can be done as an emergency, in people whose angina is so bad they are suspected of being very close to a thrombosis and heart attack.

A more recent approach is to insert a 'stent', a device like a tube of chicken wire, that holds itself open due to the springiness in the 'wire'. This is inserted via a catheter, in a similar procedure to balloon angioplasty. The artery's healing processes incorporate the stent into its wall, so that a smooth lining grows on its inside. The springiness remains, so that the vessel remains open. Stents are proving to be as successful as balloons and grafts, and the newest ones are impregnated with heart-treatment drugs that are released over months, to keep the coronary arteries open and the heart muscle healthy.

If you have had any of these operations you will be asked to take warfarin and aspirin from the time of surgery onwards, as a protection against future thromboses.

A warning

No advice on angina would be complete without a word of warning about an impending heart attack. You must never ignore pain in the chest. You must always stop and rest when it comes on. Never try to 'run through' the pain. You will only make any potential damage worse.

If the pain persists, despite stopping and taking your under-the-tongue tablet, or if it's appearing with much less exercise than it used to, then seek urgent help. You may be heading for a coronary thrombosis and myocardial infarction. Phone 999 and get an ambulance. Minutes matter, and most districts in the UK now have an emergency system just for chest pain like this, with paramedics in the ambulance who can deal with every emergency. In the meantime, swallow a whole adult aspirin. This may make a big difference to whether your heart may be damaged or not by the attack.

And a few words of advice

With the right treatment and lifestyle changes, many people with angina feel much better – so much so that they start to take up exercise again. If you do, then swim, walk, run, ski, play tennis, golf, cycle, just as you wish. But try not to be too competitive; don't push yourself to the limit to win a contest. And don't take up sports that involve sudden bursts of strength, like weight lifting, shot putting, or even competitive squash.

Sex may provoke angina, but that doesn't mean you must avoid it completely. As with any exercise, a trinitrin under the tongue beforehand may help to avoid an angina attack. A position that enables you not to lie flat can help too. Try a few pillows behind your head and upper chest.

People with angina can drive (personal use, not necessarily a job involving driving), providing the act of driving itself does not cause an attack. However, you should inform your insurer that you have angina, or otherwise the insurance may be invalid in a future crash. You will probably need a doctor's note stating you are fit to drive. Angina must also be reported to the Drivers Medical Group, DVLA, Swansea SA99 1TU: this is your responsibility, not your doctor's.

HGV drivers who develop angina must look for another job. Angina bars people from holding HGV licences, although if the angina is cured by surgery, the licence may be granted again after thorough investigation.

Your angina should not stop you flying as a passenger, but be careful to organize your trip well in advance, so that there is plenty of time at the airport and between flights. Modern air travel is no joke, and stresses of long delays and rushing from terminal to terminal can provoke angina. If your angina is severe, the airline would appreciate notification beforehand, so that they can make your journey as easy and stress-free as possible.

Holidays are fine, and just as good for people with angina as for anyone else. Avoid extremes of heat and cold, and hilly resorts where there is no alternative to walking up steps and slopes. Angina can become more of a problem when the air becomes rarefied, say, at heights above 7,000 feet, so, although the clear mountain air may be good for you, keep to the lower slopes.

Do take out health insurance when travelling abroad, as the NHS does not pay your health costs when you are out of the country. There are arrangements for emergency treatment with EU and some other countries: they are detailed in the British Department of Health booklet *T1 – The Traveller's Guide to Health*. Phone 0800 555 777 for a copy.

12

A final word – on attitude to your poor memory

It's natural to feel worried about the future after being told you have multi-infarct memory loss. You may fear this may be fatal. In fact, the life span of people with it is similar to that of people of the same age without the illness. With regard to angina, George Bernard Shaw had his first angina attacks in his forties. He lived to his nineties – in days long before there were any effective treatments. So be optimistic, and don't let the diagnosis get you down.

In fact, this advice applies to all people who find that their memories aren't what they used to be, regardless of the cause. That goes, too, for all of us who are still healthy, and whose memory is poor just because we haven't been working at it recently – which is by far the great majority of the readers of this book.

There are few memory loss sufferers who can't improve their lives. By stopping smoking, losing weight, exercising sensibly, eating healthily, drinking in moderation, getting the right attitude to stress, learning to relax, and just enjoying being alive, you can feel better and substantially improve both your quality of life and your memory at the same time.

If you are a relative or carer of someone with memory problems, let him or her lead as normal a life as possible. Don't fuss, or prevent activities that are well within his or her capabilities. Over-protection only encourages invalidism, and that is not what is wanted. The theme from you is optimism and encouragement – and the result will be a better life for you both.

Index

psychoanalysis 46–7
puberty 36–8

repetitive learning 36, 56
risk factors 107–8
Robinson, Dr Gail 20–1
Roman room 57–9

scans 27
seasonal affective disorder (SAD) 88–9
sleep 41–2
smoking 104–5
studying 42–4

subconscious memory 45
surgery 114–15

taxi drivers 12–15, 55
teenagers 85
The Knowledge 13–14
thyroid problems 73–7
toddlers 33–5

Walker, Murray 54–5
warfarin 110–11
Welsh, Leslie 1
Wilson, Dora 30–1